THE WORLD AFTER THE WAR

THE WORLD AFTER THE WAR

Charles Roden Buxton, Dorothy Frances Jebb ,Buxton

THE WORLD AFTER THE WAR

Charles Roden Buxton, Dorothy Frances Jebb ,Buxton

ISBN : 9789333111010

Reprint 2013 in India by

Isha Books
B-69, New Gupta Colony,
New DDA Market, New Delhi - 110009

Printed at : Sagar Color Scan, New Delhi.

THE WORLD AFTER THE WAR

CONTENTS

THE WORLD AFTER THE WAR

CHAPTER I

THE PICTURE

Laisser à la vérité sa simplicité parlante.

BARBUSSE.

FROM time to time we need to withdraw ourselves from the viewpoint of our particular work or study, and deliberately endeavour to survey the situation as a whole. It is a means of steadying ourselves, of avoiding excesses, of seeing things in their right proportion. Hewing our way through the forest of facts, of details, of rumours and counter-rumours, of immediate preoccupations, we cannot expect to take in the broad outlines of the landscape. To do that we must leave our axes among the trampled débris below, and climb to the mountain-top.

We who write this book have had, perhaps, an exceptional opportunity of gaining a bird's-eye view of the results of the War. During its progress we had made it our business to follow the course of political events as they were reflected in the foreign press; and in the course of 1919 each of us had the advantage of travelling repeatedly, on one errand or another, in neutral or Allied countries, and meeting men and women from every part of Europe. It was a matter of extraordinary interest to us to check and verify the facts that we had accumulated, and to learn how these had led up to the situation of the moment, from the lips of persons who had witnessed them at close quarters, and who had been themselves, in some instances, leading actors in them.

From the comparative serenity of Amsterdam or Berne, one could look out, as from a watch-tower, over the confusion and the chaos which marked the year after the Armistice.

The hope was generally entertained during the War that, when once hostilities were over, the world would begin to "settle down." Men felt that they were passing through a tremendous crisis in history; but they viewed it as a crisis which must have a definite end at no very distant date. To most it was an emergency of national defence, and to this cause they felt it right to subordinate all other considerations. To others, it seemed that interests wider than national defence were at stake—the claims of humanity, the welfare of future generations—and in defence of these interests they ran counter to the prevailing mood of the time. But all alike believed that it was an emergency for which their energies must be concentrated. With little calculation as to the future, they plunged into the battle, took the chances, and left themselves no reserves.

But they were mistaken. The crisis is not over. At the time when these lines are being written, some eighteen wars are still in progress. A whole series of revolutions has begun, to-day in Russia,

Germany, Austria, Hungary—to-morrow, it may be, further West.

Politically, the bonds of law and convention which, in spite of innumerable injustices, maintained a certain equilibrium in Central and Eastern Europe, have crumbled to pieces. Economically, the great interconnected machine of production and exchange, in which every part was needed for the working of every other part, has almost ceased to operate; and Europe sees starvation staring it in the face.

We are witnessing the terrible legacy of a War protracted too long; the old framework of Europe breaking down under the impact; the imposition of one colossal struggle upon another, of a war of classes upon a war of nations. The world has seen vast shiftings of power in the last five years, and these have accustomed it to the thought of sudden and revolutionary changes. To overthrow the old social order and create a new one in its place—regardless of the agonies which the re-birth may involve, for what are they by the side of the agonies of the War?—such is the vague but irresistible impulse which is driving the world forward along unknown and dangerous ways.

The power, and therefore the responsibility, of coping with this situation lies in the hands of four Governments, those of Britain, France, America and Japan. These virtually control, for the time being, the fate of the whole world. Yet they have shown no appreciation of the real issues which confront humanity.

The old ideas of conquest, the prejudices of class, the inveterate tradition of secrecy, still dominate their actions. The dead hand of the past throttles the living and struggling present. Even their own narrowly conceived objects seem beyond their power to attain. Impervious to the larger interests of civilization, they have shown themselves no less incapable of adapting means to ends within their own limited sphere. They have done as much to revive German militarism, as to crush it; as much to spread Russian "Bolshevism," as to suppress it. Half sceptics and half devotees of the new ideals which they profess, they are paralysed by an inconsistency from which the statesmen of earlier times were free. Yet we shall not over-estimate their responsibility. The peoples who follow and support them cannot avoid their share in it; and they themselves are often as much deceived as deceiving. History will pity, rather than execrate, these blind guides.

If we have estimated the situation rightly, it becomes evident that the emergency with which we are faced is one of a much longer duration than five years. We are probably facing a readjustment of world-conditions, comparable in its scope to the break-up of Europe which followed the Reformation and took shape in the Thirty Years' War, or to the volcanic upheavals which marked the collapse of the "Ancien Régime" in the stormy years from 1792 to 1815.

If the picture thus sketched seems exaggerated, the reason is that men's minds are still under the distorting influence of a prolonged and ingenious process of falsification. The suppression of thought, the darkening of counsel, the appeal to the emotions of fear and hatred, were deemed to be necessary for the successful prosecution of the War. And there were psychological necessities of a not less imperious character. Men had persuaded themselves that things must necessarily happen in a certain way; that sacrifices so terrible must lead to results proportionately great and noble; that the statesmen must have meant something by their assurances. These beliefs, ingrained by five years of war, remain powerful to-day. Into such a mental atmosphere the cold facts penetrate but slowly.

What we need in such a situation—so it seems to us—is first and foremost to see things as they are. We must not use up our energies in a brief effort, or waste our vitality in futile indignation. We must take stock of our position, recollect ourselves, and gain a new orientation. We must be rid of illusions. The time has come to call things by their proper names. The British people, in particular, has an extraordinary power of turning a blind eye to what it does not wish to believe. But truth is not the less truth because it is uncomfortable.

Our aim is a practical one. If we confine ourselves in this book to the endeavour to see with clear eyes the world that surrounds us to-day, we do not do so merely for the purpose of recording facts—still less for the barren satisfaction of proving the truth of our own forecasts. We do so because we believe that, before we can remedy the situation, we must understand it. Knowledge of the facts in their true proportions is the indispensable preliminary to action. It is action at which we aim; and the picture, predominantly gloomy as it needs must be, is a means and not an end. As long as the illusions of war-time continue in the countries less hardly hit by the War, there is little chance of that recovery and reconstruction for which the world is crying aloud. The mental and moral lethargy, which is creeping over our own country to-day, is a natural result of the prolonged strain of the War, followed by the removal of the stimulus of immediate danger or suffering. It is none the less a dereliction of duty, and none the less dangerous to ourselves. Either we are destined to be rapidly and rudely awakened from it by a catastrophe at home; or we shall drift back into the same attitude of indifference to the interests of other peoples, and to our relations with them, which helped to render this War possible, and which will contribute, if we revert to it, towards the making of other wars in the future.

It is the purpose of this book, then, to look the existing situation fairly in the face. It is for this reason that we do not deal with the causes of the War. We fully recognize the share of the enemy Governments in the responsibility for its outbreak. We hold that they, if successful, would probably have imposed the same kind of peace—and possibly a worse one—on their present conquerors. But the fact remains that the War itself has brought into being a new and a different world. Friend and enemy, the criminal and his victim, are involved in a common danger and a common need. The old issues have been superseded by new ones. How the worker is to live, how women and children are to be fed, how society is to be held together, how the world is to be purged of the baneful influences which drive men at each other's throats —these are the problems which dominate the chaotic present and the menacing future. It is by their attitude towards these issues that the Allied statesmen will be ultimately judged; the verdict of posterity upon the responsibility, immediate or remote, for the war of 1914, will not effect this judgment. They would not be absolved from the guilt and blindness which have marked their handling of the situation left behind by the War, even if the blame for its outbreak were finally laid upon the shoulders of William II, Admiral von Tirpitz, Count Berchtold, or M. Sazonov. As things stand, the raking over of these whitening embers only serves to distract the attention of the peoples from the issues which really concern them. The trial of a Hohernzollern, by a court composed of his enemies, is not so much a mockery of justice as a childish irrelevancy.

Our aim, then, is to see things soberly and distinctly; to disentangle from a scene of confusion the essential outlines; to give a single connected picture of the whole world-situation in its true proportions; to illustrate its real meaning in terms of simple human lives; and to show where those sources of recovery exist which will enable us to save something from the ravages of the storm.

CHAPTER II

THE BALKANIZATION OF EUROPE

And, midst this tumult, Kubla heard from far
Ancestral voices prophesying war.

COLERIDGE.

1. The Victorious Peoples.

THE closing weeks of 1918 were a time of triumph for the peoples of the victorious states. Hostilities had ceased on November 11th. Success had been won, success beyond the wildest dreams. The enemy lay prostrate at their feet. At the General Election which took place in Britain in December, the most brilliant expectations were held out to the electorate. The people had been told that victory was the culminating point to which all effort should be directed; that no thought need be given to any other consideration; that with victory were bound up, not only military success, but universal peace, the restoration of normal conditions, the revival of happiness. German militarism had but to be crushed, and a new world would arise. And now German militarism had been crushed, and the new world was rising before their eyes. The speeches of Mr. Lloyd George and his fellow Ministers were echoed by the statesmen of all the leading countries in the victorious Alliance.

But the rosy colours of the picture soon began to fade. For reasons which will appear more clearly below, prosperity did not revive. The cost of living remained as high as before, and in some cases actually rose. While there was a falling off in the volume of employment directly caused by the War, the industries of peace did not revive. The wrath of the public was turned against the "profiteers," and hasty measures were taken to check their operations. But the causes of the continued distress lay far deeper. Though the guns were silent in the main theatre of war, the conditions of war had not disappeared. British troops were still serving abroad at the beginning of 1919 in Germany, Austria, Constantinople, Salonica, the Dobruja, Albania, Transcaucasia, Palestine, Syria, Asia Minor, Mesopotamia, Persia, Siberia and Russia.

At home, the "sacred union" of classes in the War, so far from abolishing the bitterness of class feeling, had been followed by a reaction in which that bitterness was accentuated. The discharged soldier was filled with indignation on finding that the hero of the battlefield was a very different person when he doffed his khaki, and returned to the bench or the mine or the office-stool. By the end of the year, the so-called "industrial unrest"—the railway strike in Britain, the steel strike in America, the transport and engineering strikes in France—had seriously alarmed the supporters of law and order. The French Socialist Party became each month more revolutionary in tone. In Italy the internal situation was admittedly revolutionary. The weakest of the great Allies, Italy nevertheless maintained the largest army, for the simple reason that she dared not demobilise it. The "arditi," originally the picked storming troops, had become a kind of political organization, utilised by the reactionary parties to overawe the mob.

The War had not left the British Empire unaffected. Formidable risings had taken place in India and in Egypt. At the very doors of the mother-country, Ireland had risen in revolt. At the same General Election at which Britain expressed its satisfaction at the successful issue of the War, Ireland returned an overwhelming majority pledged to support an independent Irish Republic. The country was held down, under martial law, by some 100,000 British troops.

The state of the Continental Allies, however, was still more precarious. France could not forget the effect of the colossal losses of the War upon her already dwindling population. She was consumed by the fear of another attack from across the Rhine. The annexation of Alsace-Lorraine had gratified the national pride, but the feeling in the newly-acquired province was such that a military dictatorship was required to cope with it. The main feature of French politics was the resentful recognition of the fact that France, though she had made the greatest sacrifices of all, had emerged from the War unable to stand alone. Financially, she could not pay her way, and she refused to impose any fresh taxation in order to avert a dependence upon Anglo-American aid, which nevertheless filled her with irritation. She was counting upon defensive alliances with Britain and America—alliances which were wholly inconsistent with the supposed guarantees offered by the new League of Nations. About the League, indeed, her statesmen were frankly sceptical. She was particularly jealous over the position which Great Britain was obtaining in Syria and Arabia, and over the increase of Britain's relative strength at sea.

Every feature of French discontent was repeated in darker colours south of the Alps. Italy was sore and angry at the failure of her political aims. Her frontiers, it is true, had been extended abroad; but her people were starving at home. America placed a veto on some of her dearest ambitions, yet resistance was impossible, because without the American food-ships the country could not live. There was fighting from time to time with the South Slavs over the Dalmatian frontiers. In the autumn, the poet D'Annunzio led a mutinous force to the occupation of Fiume, and could not be dislodged. It was sedition, said the Italian press, comforting itself by adding that it was "idealistic" sedition. No amount of patriotic demonstrations could conceal the fact that Italy had not gained by the War, on balance, a greater accession of strength than she could have secured by negotiation without ever entering the War at all.

Two Powers alone stood out unscathed—America and Japan. Each of them had become a creditor nation, holding other nations in fee. Their increase in absolute strength was great; their increase in relative strength was greater still, owing to the destruction of their enemies and the weakening of their Allies. Yet these two great states were avowedly at daggers drawn, and glared at one another across the disputed waters of the Pacific.

Disarmament, whether partial or total, was apparently as far off as ever. Japan was arming because she feared the intrusion of America into her special preserves in China and Siberia, and resented the exclusion of her subjects from the Pacific Coast and (under the Monroe Doctrine) from Mexico. America was arming because she feared Japan. Britain was arming because America and Japan were arming; and because, in the uncertain and confused future, her power of commercial expansion, and of holding her heterogeneous Empire together, would largely depend upon the force she held in reserve—the rifles and the long-range guns by which the weight of diplomatic pressure is accurately measured. The one word which could not be used in such a world-situation was precisely that which, up to the end of hostilities, had been most commonly applied in prospect—the word "settlement."

2. Central and Eastern Europe.

If such was the condition of the principal Allied states, whose political structure at least was still intact, and who had the support of long-established traditions to guide them, what was the situation of those vast regions where kingdoms had risen and fallen, where "militarism" had been overthrown, where new nations had come to birth—that part of the world, in short, which most called for the application of the new principles of policy enunciated by President Wilson?

On the ruins of Germany, Austria-Hungary, and

Russia, a bewildering transformation had taken or was taking place. Germany had lost, partly permanently and partly for fifteen years, some 7,000,000 of her population, and some 37,000 square miles of territory. Austria and Hungary had become small agricultural countries, encircling huge half-disused capital cities. Two wholly new states had been created by the direct action of the victorious Powers—Poland and Czechoslovakia. Two other states—Roumania and Jugoslavia—had been so greatly enlarged that their pre-war dimensions seemed the mere nucleus of those to which they had now attained. Other states, again, had arisen out of the border-lands of the Czar's Empire, in consequence of the great revolutionary upheaval of 1917. Finland, Esthonia, Lettland, the Ukraine, Georgia, were the more solid of these. A less stable existence was the lot of Lithuania, of Armenia, of North Caucasia, of Siberia, of Turkestan; and of certain shadowy political entities, such as the Republic of Azerbaijan and the independent state of Arabia, testifying rather to the ingenuity of imperialist statesmen than to any indigenous growth of the national spirit. But even in the case of the new states possessing some real foundation in national consciousness, the frontiers were not finally settled; the new political unit was a rough sketch, rather than a finished picture.

The main features of this immense political transformation were described by Continental thinkers as "Balkanization." The phrase is an expressive one.

Before the War, Europe had been divided into three great regions with distinct political characteristics—the Western states; the region of great empires, embracing Austria-Hungary, Russia and the Easternmost portions of Germany; and the Balkans. In the first of these, the grievances of dissatisfied nationality, except in Ireland and Alsace, played but a small part. The central region of the three was the scene of many past injustices, and many grievous discontents in the present; but it had this at least to its credit, that it avoided the internecine wars of nationalities, and maintained freedom of trade over vast areas. The third region, the Balkans, consisted of several small states, without any firm bond to unite them, either in the form of mutual agreements, or of government from outside. Economically, each of them strove for independence and self-sufficiency, imposing high tariffs against its neighbours. They were pugnacious, mainly because their frontiers did not correspond to the boundaries of nationality, and each regarded itself as the mere nucleus of some future national state, whose limits must be ultimately decided by war. In other words, the conditions under which they lived were a denial of the principles alike of public right, of economic equality, and of self-determination. They were regarded by the greater Powers to the West, North and East as troubled waters in which the most skilful fishermen might hope to secure great prizes. In their internal politics, the problems of social progress played a secondary part; parties were divided by their belief in, or sympathy with, one or other of those Empires which, tempted by their discords, were competing for influence or for territorial aggrandisement within their borders.

All the distraction and confusion which had made the Balkans a synonym for political unrest and danger had now been reproduced, with tragic exactness, over a far greater area, and had begun to affect the life of peoples more advanced in civilization and more accustomed to order and culture. The central region of Europe was included, in a very real sense, within the frontiers of the Balkans, now moved Northwards and Westwards to the Baltic, the Oder, and the Rhine.

Of economic equality and freedom of intercourse there was not even a pretence. Under the Treaties of Peace, the states on the side of the Allies received every possible commercial privilege in the territory of their enemies—most-favoured-nation treatment, limited tariffs, right of residence and travel, free zones in ports, railway facilities, in some cases even the right to call upon an enemy state to construct canals to assist its rivals' trade. Not a single one of these rights, on the other hand, was accorded to the enemy states, who were thus left without any means of bargaining in the tariff wars which were once more being waged. The newly created states, following Balkan tradition, refused to exchange the most essential products with each other, and used their economic resources rather to damage their competitors than to benefit themselves.

Nor did the idea of "public right" fare better. It is true that the sovereignty of certain states—those regarded by Paris as hostile—was very strictly limited, but this did not mean that the rights of the small state were equal to those of the great, or that the strong were controlled in the interests of the weak. "Public right," in this sense, could only be secured by some genuine form of supernational Government, representing the interests of all the states, and capable of being called to account by the humblest of them. The new League of Nations did not constitute such a Government. It was the Allied and Associated Powers under a new name. By its constitution, a permanent majority on the Council was guaranteed to the all-powerful "Five." All power was in their hands. Not only as against the enemy, but as against their own minor Allies, they were marked off by sharp distinctions. "The *principal* Allied and Associated Powers" became a familiar phrase. It was to these alone that territories such as the German colonies, Prussian Memel, or Bulgarian Thrace, were handed over. The rest of the Allies were excluded from such privileges, as well as from all participation in the making of the Treaties of Peace. Such a form of control, instead of curbing national ambitions and economic exclusiveness, only served to encourage and stereotype them. Its most signal success during 1919 was the destruction of Soviet Hungary. It is significant of its limitations that even this object could only be gained by giving a "free hand" to one of the League's members, which happened to be on the spot and to have a direct interest, national and commercial, in the process of destruction.

3. The Principle of Nationality.

As for the principle of "nationality," it received a notable application in the setting up of new states nominally based upon ethnical considerations. But if old injustices were removed, new ones were created. The national principle was applied where it was advantageous to the Allies from a military point of view; where it promoted the interests of powerful capitalist groups, or where it could be invoked to punish an enemy. In other cases it was violated. Self-determination was refused to Ireland because it conflicted with the first of these necessities; to East Galicia because it conflicted with the second; to Bulgaria because it conflicted with the third.

The test of a genuine national settlement may be put in the form of a question—Does it leave behind it grievances so considerable that men will look forward to some future rearrangement by war? Judged by this test, the policy of the Allies conspicuously failed. Poland, Czechoslovakia, Roumania, Jugoslavia, displayed many of the characteristics of the imperial states out of whose wreck they had arisen, and whose violation of nationality had always been regarded as a menace to peace. Mr. Morgenthau, the former American Ambassador at Constantinople, early pointed out that these new states, while lacking that source of strength which comes from great industries, nevertheless were "spreading themselves out, quarrelling, weakening themselves in the process, and trying to swallow up peoples of different races and aspirations." "In many parts of Central Europe which I have recently visited," he said in September 1919, "the people are discussing trifling boundaries with far more interest than future peace." Czechoslovakia included 3½ million Germans, and large blocks of Ukrainian and Hungarian population. Its very name was invented in order to justify the incorporation in it of the Slovak race, which though ethnically allied to the Czechs, had not demanded to be united with them, and at one stage set up an independent republic in opposition to the Government of Prague. Jugoslavia, besides being troubled by the internal dissensions of Serbs, Croats, Slovenes and Montenegrins, and the chronic resistance of her Albanian subjects, had to hold down a large Macedonian population whose sympathies lay with Bulgaria, and who had been assigned to Bulgaria by a Treaty with Serbia herself in February 1912. Roumania included Bulgarian, Ukrainian, German, Hungarian and Serb populations.

Poland, however, was the outstanding example of a country which, while claiming to be a national state, was in reality an Empire. It included large districts of Posen and West Prussia, which were purely German. It held in subjection Lithuanians in the North, White Russians in the East, Ukrainians in the South-East. The Polish policy of the Allies was strategic. It aimed at driving a wedge between Russia and Germany, by means of a state of such a character that it must necessarily have quarrels with both. It was in harmony with the aims of the Polish imperialist party, with which the Allied Governments had long been in close relations; it was contrary to the aims of the moderate parties, and especially of the Socialists. We do well to rejoice over the creation of an independent Poland, and over the righting of the wrong done to that unhappy people by its partition between Prussia, Austria, and Russia. But a policy which creates a new German "irredenta," which transfers the old grievances from one side to the other, which enables Poland to inflict upon her neighbours an injustice identical in character with that which she formerly suffered at their hands, is the most poisonous gift which could possibly be bestowed upon a young state. Instead of being free to cope with its internal difficulties, among which the Jewish question occupies the first place, the new Poland finds itself committed from the first hour of its existence to a foreign policy complicated by strained relations with all its neighbours, and to the militarist and autocratic form of government which such relations will render necessary. It forms, perhaps, the most dangerous centre of unrest in Europe—dangerous to its patrons as well as to its enemies, for it forms in a sense the pivot of their European policy, and if an internal revolution should overthrow the Polish imperialists—which at the time of writing seemed probable—the whole of that policy might collapse.

If the principle of nationality had been applied with honesty, the destruction of the Central Empires would have removed some of the chief causes of conflict in Europe. There would have been mixed districts with large discontented minorities, but there would have been none in which the majority of the population laboured under a burning sense of grievance. Even, however, had the national problems been settled to the utmost extent which the mixture of population allowed, a true pacification of Europe would not have been possible unless other changes had taken place at the same time. Europe was not ripe for the vindication of nationality on a gigantic scale, without a complete alteration of its political system. The change would only have been successful if it had been accompanied by a full measure of economic equality, by the restriction or abolition of tariffs and trade restrictions, and by the definite substitution of some form of international government for the old traditions of unlimited state sovereignty. Not one of these conditions was fulfilled.

The transformation of Europe after the War was no mere shuffling of political cards. It was not merely that old European Treaties had been cast in the melting-pot, that long established understandings had been broken down. These things were but the outward forms which embodied grievous human realities—the personal misery of men and families and peoples cut adrift from their old moorings—the uncertainty about the morrow which saps the springs of sober constructive action and gives the rein to the maddest ambitions and cupidities.

4. Some Sidelights.

To give some picture of what the War has really meant to the men, women and children of this vast area, it will be useful to take a rapid survey of some of the chief areas of conflict. We shall begin on the shores of the Baltic, traverse the central heights and plateaux which form the geographical backbone of Europe, and descend to the Adriatic on the South, and the Caucasus on the South-East. But it must not be forgotten that the survey will be incomplete; a few typical examples will be picked out, almost at random, from the general confusion.

Riga, on the Baltic shore, may illustrate, as in a microcosm, the grinding backward and forward of the steam-roller of war. In 1914 it was, of course, in Russian occupation. In 1915 the Russian General Staff, forced to retreat, adopted the cruel policy of clearing out the Lettish population in order to prevent the Germans from recruiting, or profiting by the economic resources of the country. To this day, some 200,000 Letts are said to be scattered in various parts of Russia. In 1917 the Germans occupied Riga, which was placed under a Government of "Baltic barons." In November 1918 a Lettish Government of a democratic character was installed. In January 1919 Riga was captured by the Bolshevists, partly Russian and partly Lettish, and the Soviet régime began. The hunger by this time was terrible; Mr. Hoover wanted to feed the city, but the Allies refused. In May 1919 it fell before the "Baltic" militia, a force raised mainly from the German-speaking minority, and controlled by the insubordinate General Von der Golz. A "White Terror" followed, in which the mere fact of Lettish nationality was enough to secure conviction before a "Balt" court-martial. In July 1919 the Balts in their turn were driven out, and the democratic Lettish Government re-established. This Government was threatened from within by the Bolshevist tendency of the population, and attacked from without by Von der Golz and the anti-Bolshevist Russians with whom he co-operated.

Let us pass on to the central European coal-field, which embraces (to use pre-war nomenclature) the German district of Upper Silesia, the Polish districts of Dombrova and Soskovice, and the Austrian district of Teschen. The political future of this area was still undecided. Czechs and Poles disputed Teschen; the Czech miners struck work as a protest against its annexation by Poland, and threatened to take it by force. Austria's coal supply was cut off, in breach of an agreement with the Czechs, who contended that, if they lost Teschen, they would not have coal enough left for themselves. As to Silesia, the first draft of the German Treaty had handed over a large German population, without consulting them, to the Poles; the Allies then changed their minds and proposed a plébiscite; this was delayed, however, for several months. In August 1919, presumably with a view to influencing the forth-coming plébiscite, a section of the Polish population rose in revolt. They were encouraged by the success of a similar *coup de main* in Posen, where the Allies had been defied with impunity; and they were aided by armed bands from across the Polish frontier. Simultaneously, a Communist rising took place, directed against the German colliery-owners. Both the nationalist and the social risings were bloodily suppressed by the German authorities. The underfed miners were continually on strike; the employers would not concede their demands because they were uncertain as to the kind of government under which they would in future have to operate. There was an alarming fall in the output of coal at the outset of the winter.

Mr. Hoover, then engaged in trying to organize the European coal-supply, declared that the only solution was an occupation by Allied troops.

Not far distant lies East Galicia, formerly part of an Austrian province. Fierce fighting broke out between its predominantly Ukrainian population on the one side, and the Poles on the other. The Allies at first favoured the legitimate claims of the former. Great efforts were made by the Allied military missions to stop the war round Lemberg, but the country continued to be ravaged, and was reduced to something like a desert, in which life was maintained upon berries and roots. Then the fear of the irruption of Socialist ideas from the East began to influence the counsels of Paris; Poland began to be regarded as an anti-Bolshevist island; journalists began to describe the Ukrainians as "Ruthene-Bolshevist" levies which might effect a junction with the Red Army of Russia. An effort was made to secure autonomy for East Galicia within the Polish state. It was found offensive to Polish susceptibilities, and dropped. The concession was connected, presumably, with the fact that some £10,000,000 of British capital are invested in the valuable oil-wells of the district, and Allied property was deemed to be safer in Poland than in a possibly hostile Ukraine.

Our next example shall be taken from Hungary. As soon as the Armistice with that country was concluded, in November 1918, its neighbours, Czechoslovakia, Roumania, and Jugoslavia, were encouraged to invade it. The two former overstepped the limits of their "nationality" claims, and entirely ignored the remonstrances of the "Big Four" sitting at Paris. Roumania did so with some reason, for the Bukharest Foreign Office held in its pigeon-holes the Secret Treaty of August 1916, promising to Roumania a territory which included great blocks of Hungarian population. When Hungary set up a "Bolshevist" Government, the neighbouring states were not only allowed to retain what they had taken (including virtually all the mineral resources of Hungary), but were encouraged to advance to the total overthrow of the Red Army of Bela Kun. The Communist régime was overthrown, and a White Terror followed, which threw into the shade even the atrocities of the Whites in Finland. Jugoslavia alone refused to join in this attack, not because of any sense of justice or pity, but because, as she pointed out in a somewhat sarcastic Note, Paris had refused to recognize her Government; and there were other states, on whom that coveted hall-mark of respectability had been already bestowed, who were quite as capable of doing the work of the Allies.

The refusal of Jugoslavia to co-operate, and the non-recognition to which it was attributed, were to be traced back to another of those secret commitments which must have haunted the "Big Four" during the wearisome debates at Paris. For by the secret "London Treaty" of May 26, 1915, some 750,000 of the most progressive and most loyal part of the South Slav population had been assigned to Italy. This treaty was kept back from the South Slavs, but a garbled version of it became known to them, and it was the knowledge that their own legitimate claims on the Adriatic had been bartered away to Italy, which stiffened them in their refusal to concede Bulgarian Macedonia to Bulgaria—a refusal which, in October 1915, brought Bulgaria into the War.

The South Slavs might well be excused from taking a hand in the suppression of Bela Kun. They had been in armed conflict with the Italians over the question of Dalmatia; they had fought another Ally, Roumania, over the Banat of Temesvar; and they had on their hands a third quarrel with the Austrians over their Northern frontier. There had been repeated encounters over the Austrian-German towns of Klagenfurt and Marburg, the former of which had been occupied by the South Slavs in direct opposition to Allied orders.

Passing on to South Russia, to the borders of the Kiev and Volyhynia provinces, we see the extraordinary spectacle of four distinct armies, each hostile to the other three, contending for the same territory. At one moment in September 1919, within a circle with a radius of some 70 miles, the Poles were occupying Olensk; the Ukrainians under Petlyura were at Jitomir; the Red Army of the Bolshevists held Radomysl; and the "National" Army of General Denikin had just entered Kiev. The Bolshevist force, retreating Northwards from Odessa, had been allowed to pass by both Petlyura and Denikin, because each of these leaders hoped that it would attack the other.

We shall conclude our survey by a glance at the Caucasus, on the confines of European Russia and Asiatic Turkey. There was a brief space (April 27–May 31, 1918) when Transcaucasia declared itself united, and independent of Russia. In June and July it split up into three Republics, Georgia, Armenia (containing but a fragment of the Armenian race), and Azerbaijan (the Tartar region surrounding Baku). The country has immense agricultural wealth and contains, in Baku, the best oil-field in the world. Hence it became the object of special attention by both parties in the War. During most of 1919 it was occupied by 40,000 British troops. Fighting in one district or another was incessant. It broke out between Tartars and Armenians, between Armenians and Georgians, between Georgians and the "Volunteer Army" of General Denikin.

Some of these quarrels were composed by the intervention of British soldiers; but when the year closed, sporadic guerilla warfare was still in progress in the Caucasus.

5. The Multitude.

These isolated pictures may convey to the reader something of what is meant by the "Balkanization" of Europe. It is necessary to repeat that they are far from covering the whole ground. Central and Eastern Europe, from the Baltic to the Adriatic, and Eastwards across the most fertile regions of Russia to where Mount Ararat marks the border of Asia, was the scene at one stage, according to a high authority, of no less than twenty-five wars. No sooner had the flames subsided in one district than they flickered up in another. Letts, Germans, Poles, Lithuanians, Russians,

Czechs, Hungarians, Roumanians, Italians, South Slavs, Ukrainians, Georgians, Armenians—every one of these peoples was engaged in fighting, some of them on several different fronts, during this year of chaos. Armies surged to and fro, hastily improvised, appearing and disappearing, fighting for some coveted strip of territory, for the defence of their homes, for the destruction of some dreaded rival, for the chance of political recognition in some unknown future. Meanwhile the masses of the common people, trampled and robbed by the contending forces, confused by the conflicting orders of paper Governments and General Commands, of visible guerilla chieftains and remote, intangible "Allies," ignorant of why or how, conscious only that their lives and property were becoming daily less secure, and their diet more sparse and uneatable, awaited in blind endurance the next blow of their unintelligible fate.

We have taken no account in this rapid survey of the many points of friction which did not lead to fighting. But the actual armed conflicts must be pictured against a background of discontent and misery too widespread and confused to be summed up in any brief description. Some conception of it may be gained from a mere minor incident which was, nevertheless, the cause of poignant distress—the dispersion of prisoners of war. Ten months after the main hostilities were over, there were still 800,000 German prisoners in France, Britain, Belgium, Serbia, and Roumania; 300,000 Russians in Germany, and 72,000 in France, the latter having gone as allies and remained as captives with a view to being used to fight for General Denikin; 110,000 Bulgarians in France, Serbia, and Greece; while 50,000 Czechs, taken prisoners by the Russian Armies, who had first fought against the Bolshevists, and then refused to do so on the discovery that they were being used as the catspaw of the counter-revolutionary generals, were still refused a passage home to their country. But this special injustice, with its innumerable personal anxieties and bereavements, was but a fraction of the human suffering which the War had left behind it. There was hardly a country in Europe, on whichever side it had fought—or even if it had not fought at all—where deep-seated resentments and grievances had not been sown. The wonder was that in so many different cases and under so many different forms, from the Rhine to the Pacific, and from the White Sea to the Mediterranean, men still retained the will and the physical energy to take up arms.

The universal unrest was but the symptom of a profound mental turmoil. The War had given rise to portentous psychical effects—effects which science has not yet been able to measure or describe, because the nervous strain which produced them had no parallel in previous experience. Any war on so gigantic a scale as that of 1914–1918 must necessarily have caused a tearing asunder of old ties, an increased indifference to the taking of life, a drift towards violent methods. But the strain had been intensified tenfold by the length to which the War had been prolonged, and the unjust and reckless settlement which had followed it. Men oscillated between the extremes of lassitude on the one hand and feverish energy on the other. A profound cynicism, a disbelief in justice, became the normal atmosphere in which the European mind moved. In the minds of the more ignorant populations a kind of blind rage was generated, seeking instinctively for some scape-goat to expiate the wrongs of which it was conscious, but whose authors it could not identify. The most sinister form assumed by this feeling was the revival of Anti-Semitism, which recalled the strange outbreaks of witch-burning that followed the miseries of the Thirty Years' War. The persecution and massacre of the Jews broke out afresh. At one moment they were the "traitors"; at another the "profiteers"; at another the "Bolshevists."

The fact was that, whether or not it was necessary to crush completely the German military machine, it was certainly impossible to crush it, so to speak, in a watertight compartment. While it was being destroyed, a hundred other things were being destroyed in the process. The political and moral foundations of European life were crumbling to pieces.

CHAPTER III

THE NEW BALANCE OF POWER

He looked on Europe's dying hour
Of fitful dream, and feverish power.

ARNOLD.

1. "Paris."

IT was not easy to find any connecting links, any established relationships, any principle of order, in the strange phantasmagoria which has been described in the preceding chapter. In theory, "Paris" was the arbiter of the destinies of the struggling peoples. And "Paris" was itself conceived as the temporary shape of what was to crystallize ultimately into a formal League of Nations. It was at once the liquidator, the trustee, and the future board of directors. But "Paris" itself was frequently defied, sometimes by Allies such as Poland and Roumania, sometimes by enemy *condottieri* like Von der Golz in the Baltic Provinces and Mustapha Kemal in Central and Eastern Anatolia. Its decrees, too, were capricious, and not easily reconciled with one another. In so far as any general policy underlay the operations of the three or four statesmen who issued their fiats from the French capital, it appeared to rest upon the conception of two classes or categories of states, the friendly and the hostile; on the one hand, those which had fought on the side of the Allies, or had been created by them, or were amenable to pressure by them; on the other hand, those which had fought against them, those which, like Georgia and the Ukraine, were suspect on account of their previous relations with the principal enemy, and those which, like Russia and Hungary, were believed to constitute a menace to social order outside their own frontiers. The principle on which the friendly class was selected, had been at first comparatively simple. The design was to form a rampart of states, Poland, Czechoslovakia, Jugoslavia, with an additional outwork in Roumania, in order to cut off Germany's expansion towards Asia. But the principle became afterwards complicated by another, that of creating a "sanitary cordon" to check the infection of Socialism from the East; and the application of the new principle became increasingly difficult as the infection spread, and the cordon had to be hastily shifted Westwards. When, for instance, Communism took root in Hungary, Roumania ceased to form part of the "cordon," and her claims accordingly found less support at Paris than those of Czechoslovakia, which might still, it was hoped, arrest the spreading germ. The new principle had another important result. A kind of competition in "anti-Bolshevism" began among the states that were striving for recognition at the hands of the Great Allies. Esthonia, Lettland, Lithuania, the Ukraine, each in turn tried to curry favour with these Powers by representing itself as the indispensable outpost against the dreaded encroachment.

2. The League of Nations.

We may be met at this point by the argument that we have ignored the new League of Nations. That, it may be said, was the new principle of order, the great achievement of Allied policy. We cannot accept this view. We are dealing with things as they are, and not with paper undertakings, however solemn in form. We fully recognize the gain represented by the currency which has been given to the old idea of a League of Nations. The possible development of that idea is one of the forces of recuperation to which we shall make allusion in our final chapter. Every effort must be made to realize in practical action the many hopeful features of the new "Covenant" which has been embodied in the Peace Treaties. But the concrete terms of the Treaties of Peace, and the actual work which the League will be called upon to do, must count for more than embryonic principles which may take many different forms according to the development of international relations.

Moreover, it is only in a technical sense that the Covenant forms part of the Peace Treaties. Germany, Austria, Hungary, Bulgaria, Turkey, are not admitted to the League. Nor, of course, is Russia. And its constitution is such that their admission to it, on terms corresponding to their place in the world, is rendered almost impossible. The predominant power is given to America, Japan, and the Western Powers of Europe; and this arrangement takes on a more sinister aspect when it is realized that all the newly arisen revolutionary or socialistic states are shut out from participation in the League.

The real bearing of the proposal of a League of Nations on the peace settlement can only be appreciated in conjunction with the other provisions of the Treaties. These transfer whole populations against their will to alien forms of government, and consign the enemy peoples to a state of economic servitude. They impose upon those peoples a drastic and immediate process of disarmament, while their enemies are left in full enjoyment of their naval and military strength, subject to a promise that at some unspecified date the Council of the League will " formulate plans for consideration and adoption."

Now the immediate task of the League—whatever its later developments may be—is to guarantee the stability of these essentially unstable conditions. This is the most important of the reasons which influenced America in her refusal (November 1919) to be bound by any of the more substantial obligations of the "Covenant." Such a task is one which no true League of Nations could execute; and any League which endeavoured to execute it, even with the best intentions, would find itself compelled to become a great militarist organization, destitute of that healing spirit of reconciliation which alone can make it an instrument of progress. It would in fact become one of the players in what President Wilson once described as " the great game, now for ever discredited, of the Balance of Power." The League does not redeem the terms of the Treaties; the terms degrade the League.

And there is another factor in the situation which closely affects the value of the League of Nations as hitherto outlined. This is the defensive alliance between the United States, Great Britain, and France which President Wilson and Mr. Lloyd George undertook in 1919 to propose to their respective Parliaments, though, at the time of writing, its acceptance was still a matter of speculation. Such an alliance is inconsistent with President Wilson's principle that "there can be no leagues or alliances, or special covenants and understandings, within the general and common family of the League of Nations" (speech of September 27, 1918). It is indeed a proof that the League is not regarded as providing a guarantee against aggression.

Lastly, in the very matters which are laid down in the "Covenant" as the League's special spheres of action, the League has been already ignored. Colonial "mandates" had been parcelled out among the victorious Powers—the principle being applied to enemy territory alone—even before the League was formed. And the Anglo-Persian Agreement of 1919 had made Persia wholly dependent upon Great Britain, instead of looking for her protection to the League.

The fact is that the "great game," so far from being for ever discredited, was being actively played during the year following the War.

The political system of Europe, in so far as any such system was emerging at all, was the old "Balance of Power" in a new form. That ancient principle of foreign policy had been consistently advocated by the *Times* in England; and with more brilliance and logic by the Chauvinist press of France, which had poured open scorn on the new-fangled principles of "nationality" and "public right." The phrase is meaningless, of course, if literally interpreted; but it is sufficiently clear if taken in its accepted interpretation, as meaning the greatest possible tilting of the balance in one direction, or in other words, an overwhelming preponderance of power. What gave a new form to the "balance" now established, was that it was designed to resist, not one dangerous force, but two—the resentment of beaten enemies and the march of revolutionary Socialism.

The real power of the new combination was wielded, during the year following the Armistice, by four states, Great Britain, America, France, and Japan—the only fully-armed Powers still standing erect amid the ruins—with a large group of satellites. The composition of this group varied from time to time, but Poland, Czechoslovakia, and Jugoslavia were its most valuable members.

A more equivocal position had to be assigned to Italy and Roumania. The former had claims which could not be satisfied; she was in a state of thinly-veiled war with Jugoslavia; and she was from time to time coquetting with Germany. Roumania had begun by quarrelling with Jugoslavia over the possession of the Banat of Temesvar. She then refused to accept the frontier with Hungary which was laid down in the Allied Armistice (November 3, 1918), and successfully insisted upon a more extended occupation of territory. She finally marched upon Buda-Pesth in flat defiance of "Paris." The step was not unconnected with the fact her representatives had already shaken off the dust of the Peace Conference from their feet, as a result of their failure to secure the execution of the Secret Treaty of August 1916, between Roumania and the Allied Governments. None the less, Roumania still constituted an island of capitalist domination in the increasingly "Bolshevist" South-Eastern corner of Europe, and as such could still be regarded as, potentially at any rate, an important factor in the "balance."

Such was the combination of states whose function we have now to examine. It may be viewed under its two separate aspects—the holding down of Germany and her allies, and the resistance to revolutionary Socialism.

3. The Treaties of Peace.

In so far as it was directed to the holding down of Germany and her allies, it found expression in the Treaties of Peace. These embodied the military results of the War. Their effect on Europe in general has been described in the last chapter. What we have here to recall is their primary purpose—the crushing of the hostile states. This purpose was attained with a completeness perhaps unparalleled in history.

During the course of the War, while its issue was still uncertain, the statesmen on both sides were careful to repudiate the idea of "crushing" the enemy. Nothing was further from their thoughts, they said, than to repeat the fatal mistake which Prussia made when she crushed France in 1871. It was German militarism, and not Germany, that they were resolved to destroy. The exaction of indemnities, the endeavour to obtain not merely compensation for damage but recoupment of the expenses of the War, was specifically condemned. But the military successes of 1918 swept all these coy reservations away. The motto "victory first, then generosity" was forgotten. The extreme Chauvinists from whom the better part of public opinion had turned with some repulsion during the War, the men who had demanded that we should "hew down the pillars and sow the foundations with salt," now found themselves the exponents of the mood of the hour. The example of Prussia in 1871, instead of being upheld as a warning, was applauded as an example. The Treaties of Peace embodied, it is true, certain clear gains. They set up an independent Poland and an independent Czechoslovakia. They embodied the principle of plébiscite—though not its impartial application—for certain disputed areas. They rendered lip-service, at least, to the conception of a League of Nations. Territories which in former days would have been annexed without further to-do, were now placed under temporary occupation, or handed over to the Allied and Associated Powers conjointly, or committed in trust to this or that power as a "mandatory" of the League, or placed under an International Commission. These things represented, as far as they went, tangible improvements on earlier peace settlements; they were the actual gains secured by the advance of modern democracy. It is true also that certain protests were raised by men of liberal mind who had supported their Governments during the War, in the belief that some principle other than that of conquest would be applied to the settlement. The most distinguished of these was the Reformist Socialist, Signor Bissolati. But it was in vain that they protested. As well might a man order an omelette, and then abuse the cook for breaking eggs. The general lines of Allied policy had been too clearly laid down in the secret agreements made during the War. In the privacy of the chancelleries, relieved from the necessity of throwing sops to public opinion, the statesmen had expressed their real aims with precision and in detail.

The net result of the Treaties was to crush the hostile group of states almost beyond recognition, and to place the friendly group in a position of such overwhelming military superiority that they could trample at will upon their former enemies. These were rendered practically defenceless by enforced disarmament, while the victors remained fully armed. The British, American, and Japanese navies dominated the seas.

The territory of the beaten group was amputated on all hands, large blocks of German, Austrian, Hungarian, and Bulgarian population being handed over to the rule of their enemies. Of the economic provisions, which we shall discuss more fully below, it is enough to say that they had the effect of ruining the enemy states as commercial rivals. Large quantities of their agricultural stock and railway material, and the main part of their merchant shipping, were handed over to the victors. Their industry was deprived of its main sources of supply, and they were cut off from free economic access to the outer world. On the various international bodies through which the new League of Nations was to exercise its functions, they were unrepresented. Belgium, Greece, and Brazil sat on the controlling Council of a League from which Germany, Austria, and Russia were altogether excluded.

4. The World outside Europe.

It was not only in Europe that the "balance" was thus tilted. The change in the relative strength of the two groups was even more conspicuous in Africa, in Asia, and in the Pacific. The oversea possessions of Germany were handed over to the victorious Powers conjointly. They proceeded to bestow upon themselves the "mandates" which, in theory, should have been dealt out by the League of Nations. The terrible effects of the War on African soil—the mortality among native troops and native carriers, the confusion created in the native mind, the inter-tribal wars which the military operations had stimulated—were intensified by the spectacle, so dangerous from the point of view of "white" predominance, of one European Power fighting, defeating, and plundering another with the aid of African mercenaries.

Britain declared a protectorate over Egypt and France over Morocco. France obtained Syria and Cilicia, while Italy and Greece occupied other Turkish territories. Britain annexed Cyprus, occupied Mesopotamia, and created a new Arab state in which her influence was the main factor. She concluded a Treaty with Persia by which she obtained the political, military, and economic control of a land in which she had formerly been faced with the formidable competition of Russian bayonets and Russian diplomacy. From the Cape of Good Hope to India, she succeeded in eliminating every serious foreign rivalry, whether in German East Africa, Turkish Arabia, or Persia. While the cohesion of the Empire as a whole was seriously diminished, its territory and its area of control were greatly extended.

In Eastern Asia and the Pacific Japan was left in a position of almost unassailable superiority. Her demands upon China, amounting in the aggregate to financial, military, and economic control over nearly the whole of the Celestial Empire, were accepted without effective challenge by the rest of the Allies. She was in firm occupation of the former German territory of Kiao-chau. She had effectively annexed Korea. Her position in Manchuria was finally established, and she was in virtual occupation of Siberia, East of Lake Baikal. Under the Peace Treaty with Germany, she received in addition the whole of Germany's so-called "rights" in the province of Shantung, commanding the routes which connect the capital with South China, and embracing a Chinese population of about 36 millions.

5. The Socialist Wave.

We have now to view the new combination of power under another aspect. The Allies, as we have seen, were faced with the problem of counterbalancing, not merely any possible revival of the strength of their late enemies, but also the spread of a new and, as some of them held, more dangerous force—revolutionary Socialism.

The social upheaval began with the Russian Revolution of March 1917, which deposed the Tsar and led to the establishment of the Kerensky Government. Its first extensions took place, naturally, within the borders of Russia. The Ukraine established (December 15, 1918) a Social Democratic Government of a moderate character, which was overthrown (February 5, 1919) by the Bolshevist movement—primarily an internal and native one, but fomented and assisted by Red Armies from Great Russia in the North. The example of the Ukraine was followed by the new Republics of Georgia and Armenia, both of which established Social Democratic Governments, and in different forms by Poland and Finland. The Kerensky régime was superseded, in November 1917, by the "Bolshevist" or Communist régime. The main source of revolutionary ideas became the Soviet Republic, with its centre at Moscow, and its circumference alternately expanding and contracting as the fortunes of war swayed this way and that.

The social upheaval was destined, however, to spread far beyond the borders of the Tsar's Empire. Its next great extension occurred at the time of the Armistice (November 1918). Germany and Austria both expelled their dynasties, and became Socialist Republics of a moderate type. In March 1919, the stop-gap Government of Count Karolyi, despairing of any other solution of a problem rendered almost insoluble by blockade and foreign intervention, handed over the government of Hungary to the Communist Party led by Bela Kun, whose Government lasted till it was overthrown in August 1919 by the pressure of the Allies' blockade. The Allies promised to support the Social Democratic Government of Peidl. This, however, was violently ejected after a few days by the Roumanian Army, which occupied Buda-Pesth, and promoted, or connived at, the dictatorship of a Hapsburg Archduke. He in his turn was repudiated by the Allies, and his brief sway was followed by the reactionary rule of his monarchist and anti-Semitic henchmen. In Czechoslovakia, a Social Democratic Premier, Tusar, took office in the summer of 1919. The Socialists were beginning to play a part in the politics of Jugoslavia, and for a few days (August 1919) a partly Socialist Government was in power at Belgrade. The revolutionary movement was rapidly gathering force in Roumania. In Bulgaria, where Socialism has always been stronger than in other Balkan countries, the extreme or "Narrow" Socialists obtained striking victories at the elections of September 1919, securing 47 seats. In Turkestan, Siberia, and even in the Far East, particularly in Korea, the movement was by no means negligible.

It was above all between the Volga and the Rhine that the leaven was working. Count Karolyi said in an interview that "Social Democracy—call it what you will—has become a necessity in the East of Europe." Even West of the Rhine, in countries as far apart as Sweden, Holland, Portugal, Switzerland, and Italy, there were movements of a sufficiently revolutionary character to give grave alarm to the ruling classes. Everywhere the struggle between nations was being complicated by the struggle between classes, which had now become " practical politics " for the first time since 1848, and on an infinitely greater scale.

The many and varying forms assumed by the new social upheaval had this in common, that all alike were frowned upon by the statesmen at Paris. They were part of the rebellious and dangerous forces against which the new Balance of Power was directed. The Allies did not confine their hostility to the more extreme forms of Socialism. The treatment meted out to the Moderate Socialist Governments of Germany and Austria was as severe as that which would have been imposed upon an unrepentant militarism. In Hungary, the Social Democratic and Labour Government of Peidl, with whose representatives the Allies had negotiated just before the fall of Bela Kun (August 1919), received no more mercy at their hands, when it came into power, than Bela Kun himself. The Socialist Governments of the Ukraine and Georgia were treated with hardly less suspicion and hostility than those which had arisen in enemy countries. The Allies did their utmost, by economic pressure, to render intolerable the lot of all Socialist states—if we except Czecho-slovakia, where their policy could not easily be altered at short notice, and where the Socialist tendency of the Government was too feeble to influence the country's foreign policy, or impair its value from the military point of view. The Polish Socialist Government was overthrown, according to the common belief, because the

Allies refused to meet Poland's need for supplies so long as it remained in power. The Letts were told that the Allies would cut off their food imports if they set up a Socialist Government.

But perhaps the most striking proof of the Allies' hostility, even to Moderate Socialism, was their attitude towards the first Revolution in Russia—that of March 1917. Later, when "Bolshevism" was the enemy, it became customary to look back with retrospective admiration upon Kerensky, to contrast his moderation with Lenin's excesses, to denounce the Bolshevists as the destroyers of "genuine" Socialism, and actually to claim that British troops were being sent to fight against Russia in order to restore the earlier Socialist régime, and in particular the Constituent Assembly which had been elected under it. These assertions, however, were in fact a mere afterthought. While Kerensky was actually in power—and in spite of the fact that he represented an Allied country which had made gigantic sacrifices in the War—he received no favour from the Governments of Western Europe. His appeal to them to make peace, his demand for the restatement of terms on the basis of "no annexations and no indemnities," were resolutely rejected; his warnings of Russia's imminent collapse were ignored; and he was forced, by the threat that otherwise all economic support would be withdrawn, into a disastrous offensive which led directly to the downfall of his Government, the November Revolution, and the Peace of Brest-Litovsk.

After this failure, the Allies had yet another chance of proving the sincerity of their claim to be the friends of the Russian people. The majority of the members of the Constituent Assembly, to which they had pointed as the real organ of democratic Russia, and over whose dissolution they had shed so many tears, formed a Government at Ufa (September 1918) in opposition to that of Lenin. Yet so far from supporting this Government, the Allies refused even to recognize its representatives abroad. They permitted Admiral Kolchak to dissolve it (November 1918), to imprison its members, to put some of them to death, and to proclaim himself a dictator.

The complaint was seriously made that it was impossible to know what kind of Government was really approved by "Paris." The question became a most practical one for those who were striving, at any cost, to reconstruct some form of order in Central and Eastern Europe. Socialism was evidently proscribed. What about a Government of the Liberal type, composed of men such as Count Karolyi in Hungary or Prince Max of Baden in Germany—men with the old ideas of property, but quicker in sympathy and yielding more readily to the demand for sweeping changes? These, one would have thought, would have commended themselves to the professors of ordered democracy. But these seemed no better in their sight, and fared no better at their hands. What then? Admiral Kolchak? The Archduke Joseph? Yes—here at first it seemed that approval might be won. But when faced with these avowed representatives of the old régime, the Allies recoiled. They remembered their previous professions. They were "fighting for democracy." The result was a compromise. Admiral Kolchak was recognized, provided he would tie himself down by the promise that he would summon, some day, some sort of Constituent Assembly. Again, the Archduke was rejected, but his entourage, without the man himself, were supported in their efforts to form a Government. Anti-Socialism became more and more the prime object. When Socialism really raised its head, the Allied statesmen appeared to feel that Militarism was the better after all.

6. Soviet Russia.

It was against "Bolshevism," of course, that the main efforts of the Allies were directed. Their profession was that it was this form of Socialism, not Socialism in general, that they were opposing. In point of fact, the excesses of Russian Communism were exploited to create a popular bogey, in order that this in its turn might be used to discredit all forms of Socialism. The majority of the Allied newspapers were ready enough to second the efforts of the Governments. "Bolshevist" became as opprobrious a nickname as "pro-German" had been during the War.

This, however, was but an incident. The use of Allied power which exceeded all others in importance, so far as the new social movement was concerned, was the war against Soviet Russia. The attitude of the Allied Governments was thus officially expressed in a Note of the Supreme Council to Germany, requesting co-operation in the blockade of Bolshevist Russia (October 1919): "The openly expressed hostility of the Bolshevists directed against all Governments, and the programme published by them of an international revolution, constitute a grave danger for the national security of all Powers. Every increase in the capacity of the Bolshevists for resistance increases this danger, and it would, on the other hand, be desirable that all peoples which seek to restore peace and social order should unite in order to fight against it." The methods used against Germany and her Allies were replaced by a much simpler process. Instead of disarmament by Treaty, the Allies engaged in armed invasion, and the fomenting of civil conflict. Instead of territorial amputation in the alleged interests of nationality, they supported the parties whose aim was to restore a centralised empire, as the best means of upholding the threatened cause of property and order. Instead of a network of economic and financial clauses, they fell back on the cruder method of blockade. Only in one respect were their methods identical; Germany and Russia alike were excluded from all participation in the new League of Nations which was to inaugurate the reign of law.

During 1919, the operations of the Allies against the Russian Soviet Republic were conducted on a great scale from Vladivostok to Riga, from Murmansk to Odessa, from Archangel to Astrakhan. British forces, in spite of promises of withdrawal, were still engaged in North Russia in the late summer. The armies of Admiral Kolchak and General Denikin (the former of whom, after making himself "Supreme Ruler" by a *coup d'état*, afterwards placed himself under the orders of the latter) were operating on the borders of European and Asiatic Russia, and in the Ukraine. They were being supported by the Allies with finance, munitions, and a small number of troops. A Roumanian advance was being supported on the South-West, a Polish advance on the West. Further North, the vast plan of campaign was being rounded off by the organization of a composite army under the Russian General Yudenich, including large numbers of German soldiers in Russian uniforms. There was fitful support from the various border states—Finland, Esthonia, Lettland, Lithuania, and the Ukraine—but it was unreliable, because though they feared Bolshevism, they feared even more the centralizing and imperialist policy of the Kolchak-Denikin faction. In the Far East, at the time of writing, the struggle continued only in the form of guerilla warfare in the frontier regions of Russia and North-Eastern China. A large Japanese force was stationed in Eastern Siberia.

7. Unstable Equilibrium.

We have now reviewed the methods by which the new Balance of Power was being established during the year 1919. The chief Allied Governments, on the surface at any rate, presented an imposing array of force. They held the field. They wielded the economic resources of the world. They had in their hands the power of life and death over whole continents. Each of them controlled a vast military and administrative machine. Their power over men's minds, as exercised for example by the control of news from Russia, still remained very great, in spite of the relaxation of the censorship.

Yet "Paris" no longer stood for what it had stood for at the end of 1918. It was then looked upon as a seat of empire—almost as the "machine" or platform from which, in classical tragedy, the gods appeared at the end of the play, to unloose the knot which no human ingenuity could untie. Gradually, however, it proved to be something less than omnipotent. The limitations of its power became more evident from month to month. It received blows in the house of its friends—Poland, Roumania, Japan—more damaging than the verbal assaults of its helpless enemies. Stability, in short, was as yet unachieved. The old order had been destroyed, but no new one had been set up in its place; the peoples which had been crushed and broken in the War were labouring under a sense of intolerable injustice; a vast social struggle had been superimposed upon the struggle of nations; and the future was clouded with uncertainty. Competition in armaments between the Allies; a German-Russian coalition to counterbalance the League of the Western and extra-European Powers; monarchist reaction in one country, and the spread of revolution in another; wars of violated nationality, and wars for the reconquest of economic power—these were the dangerous possibilities which still darkened the horizon of Europe.

CHAPTER IV

THE ECONOMIC COLLAPSE

Quicquid delirant reges, plectuntur Achivi.

HORACE.

1. The Common People.

WE have hitherto confined our survey to the political transformation which followed the War. This transformation, however, was accompanied by catastrophic changes in the economic sphere. Over large areas of Europe and Asia, the machinery by which men are fed, clothed, warmed and housed had broken down.

We reach down here to the human realities which underlie the shiftings of political power. Measured in terms of simple human lives, the economic collapse which followed the War is an event of greater import than the fall of Governments and the clash of armies. These things leave many millions unaffected. But hunger, cold, disease—and the anxieties and miseries of the struggle against them—cross almost every threshold, and overshadow the lives of men, women and children who are indifferent to, if not totally ignorant of, the things which fill the minds of statesmen and generals.

But just because the numbers affected are so incalculable, we fail to feel their significance. "The brain is made to grasp infinity," says a modern writer, "but the heart is not."

A single case of suffering may be presented with some vividness, but it gives no conception of the vast number of cases of which it is typical. On the other hand, statistics of rationing, of milk shortage, of the spread of disease, though they convey the extent of the evil, fail to yield any strong impression of the poignancy of the individual cases. Moreover, men have supped so full with horrors during the War that their palate has become jaded. The cry of hollow-eyed women and shivering children in Prague or Buda-Pesth, in Lodz or Vienna or Petrograd, sounds "like a tale of little meaning, though the words are strong." Yet that cry has been wrung from our fellow-creatures by a distress for which we ourselves are in great part responsible; and our first duty is to make the deliberate effort of imagination which is needed to give meaning to the tale.

"There is no actual starvation," reported an eye-witness from Poland, "but the people are living on vegetables and greenstuffs, and in the more remote spots many are surviving on roots, herbs, and berries" (*September* 1919). Such reports were confirmed by many other observers. "Inquests on many victims of death from hunger reveal in the stomach the presence of sand and wood" (*June*).

"One of the chief officials who has just returned from Poland and Lithuania gave me the most harrowing accounts of what he saw. Hundreds of thousands of the people are getting as their daily sustenance *a dish of soup consisting of water with one-third of a medium-sized potato in it.* He saw women and children fighting like wild beasts for food. In private houses he found men, women and children lying, generally stark naked, on a bed, too weak to move, dying or dead of hunger. If he asked them their names or put other questions to them he seldom got any reply but 'Bread, bread'" (*May*).

Mr. McDougall, Chief Commissioner of Live Stock for Scotland, appointed by the British Government to investigate food conditions in Germany, described a load of "rotten and putrid" potatoes which he saw being prepared for sale in the poorer districts of Berlin: "No farmer in Britain would dream of attempting to give this load of potatoes to any animal on his farm. . . . It was with difficulty that one could believe these potatoes . . . could be eaten by any human creatures; only the pangs of direct hunger would make their consumption possible" (*British White Paper*, 1919, *Cmd.* 280, *published July* 1919).

The Berlin correspondent of the *Daily Express* wrote: "Thirty per cent. of the German women die in confinement. Thirty per cent. of the children born to married mothers die, and 50 per cent. of those born to unmarried mothers. I have encountered dozens of children two years of age who have never tasted milk" (*May* 5, 1919).

Of Vienna, Drs. Hilda Clark and Ethel Williams reported in June 1919: "You never see a normal child in the streets. . . . There are no toddlers; children of three or even four have still to be carried by their mothers." "I was four days in Vienna," says one of them, "before I saw a child play." Mrs. Vorse, who made a special investigation of food conditions in Vienna, wrote:

"One day I was in a restaurant, and a flower vendor approached my table and saw a bit of ham rind I had left on my plate as unfit to eat. She came close, whispering, and asked if I intended to leave that bit. When I said that I did, she stretched out her hand and grabbed it" (*July 2nd*). A correspondent thus described the arrival of a party of underfed Vienna children in Switzerland, where large numbers of them were received for several weeks at a time by the hospitable Swiss :— "The little army formed itself up and marched silently and painfully out of the station into the street flanked with well-filled shops. Presently they passed a confectioner's, from which a smell of baking emerged, and whose windows were gay with sugared dainties. With one accord they stopped and gazed, their eyes hungry and yet sad, like the eyes of a dog that has been constantly beaten" (*October 28th*).

It is not difficult to fill up the picture of family life under conditions such as those described above—the daily struggle of the mother, the perpetual ailing of the children, the absence of childhood's vitality and brightness, the deepening shadow of anxiety.

Writing of Czechoslovakia, a traveller thus described the children :—"Tiny faces, large dull eyes overshadowed by mighty, puffed, rickety foreheads, their small arms just skin and bone, and above the crooked legs with their dislocated joints, the swollen, pointed stomachs of the hunger-œdema. Scarcely one amongst all these children can keep its head erect" (*June 8th*).

Of the vast area of the distress, some idea may

be conveyed by turning our glance to the extreme South-Western corner of Europe. Many of the Armenians in the Erivan district of the Caucasus, says a traveller, "subsist on grass and leaves and have had no normal food for weeks. Beyond question, bodies recently buried have been dug up and the flesh torn off and eaten by starving people. . . . . Children I knew who could run about when I was working there last year now cannot walk, and people stuff into their mouths anything into which they can dig their teeth, just to try and stop the craving" (*June 25th*). Of the same district we read :—"The streets are full of weeping and begging. I can certainly say I have never seen a smile in this place—just people crying all the time 'Ajam! Ajam' (I am hungry)."

The misery of insufficient clothing was hardly less than that of insufficient food. A British doctor wrote from Hungary that the worn-out blankets in the hospitals "can no longer be disinfected. . . . For want of washing material, the mattresses are soiled. . . . The new-born child is wrapped in old rags . . . and at the end of ten days is sent home literally naked, mother and child being generally fated to die of cold and hunger. . . . Bandages as well as cotton wool (in the Balassa Hospital) are made from paper, and answer very badly. . . . The quality of the clothes is very bad, because only paper is to be had. The swaddling clothes for infants are half paper, half cotton, and are bad for the babies' skins, and useless after three washings."

At some large hospitals at Cracow, we are told, "they have now no baby clothes left, and the babies are wrapped in old pillow-cases and such like makeshifts" (*June*).

"The condition of children in Russia," said a well-known Russian lady, "is something atrocious. Lack of food and absence of clothing and linen, as well as of most necessary drugs, causes an increase of mortality, which in some places reaches 95 per cent. . . . The *new-born are wrapped up in old dirty rags which cannot be washed,* as there is no soap. . . . Last winter, owing to the lack of fuel, children got frozen noses, ears, arms, and legs even in the children's homes" (*August*). In Czechoslovakia "two thousand crowns have to be paid for a suit of clothes, and the result is that the population is going about clad in sacks. Shirts, vests, socks, practically do not exist" (*June*). In some Roumanian districts the peasants were entirely without clothes, and were making "suits" out of leaves. In the Slovak and Ruthene districts of the former Austro-Hungarian Empire, "many children at the present time are almost entirely destitute of clothing. The women are reduced to the necessity of cutting up bedclothes to make rough garments to protect themselves and their families from the ravages of the intense frost which is now prevailing" (*November*).

Disease followed hard on the steps of famine. Famine and fatigue produced a condition of lowered resistance to infection; absence of soap, linen, sheets, disinfectants, medicines, and medical appliances favoured its spread. The Central Bureau for the combating of disease in Eastern Europe published an appeal in October, pointing out that Poland, the Ukraine, Roumania, and Serbia were suffering in an equal degree from the plague of spotted typhus, which had become pandemic. "The circle is closing in ever closer round Central Europe, the danger approaches ever nearer to the Western States." The hospitals of Eastern Europe became, according to the International Red Cross, "simply foci of epidemic diseases." It is needless to add that the suffering in the hospitals themselves was intense. Patients would get out of bed, when dangerously ill, to protect themselves from the cold by walking about. "At one hospital visited," wrote a British doctor from Hungary, "there was only about two cwt. of coal in the cellar. At other hospitals, none. Consequently beds are not available, and central heating of the buildings will not be possible when the weather gets cold in November. Coal shortage also affects tuberculosis dispensaries, central disinfecting stations, and schools" (*September*). The most painful operations had to be performed without anæsthetics.

Not only physical health, but even elementary morality, began to crumble under the unnatural stress of prolonged suffering. An eye-witness reported how a woman, after waiting for many hours outside a shop, frozen and famished, for the chance of obtaining some scraps of food, killed another woman with a blow from a bottle, for taking her place in the queue. An account given by a Russian writer applies equally to other countries. He explains (in the Danish *Politiken*, April 23, 1919) that after a time the spectacle of misery ceases to make any appeal to sympathy. It only avails to make the instinct of self-preservation more keen. "At the sight of those who are more miserable, people only think how they themselves must make provision to escape a similar fate. They must see to it that they collect more foodstuffs; they must take care to hide them still more effectively. . . . Hopelessness is the feeling that dominates all and everything. And it is no doubt this feeling that there is no way out, that each day is so changing the character of the people. And when one considers that the character of children and young people is being formed in this morass, one shudders at the thought of the probable consequences." It was no wonder that the peasant hoarded, and the profiteer clutched his profits. Parents stole to save the lives of their starving children, and children to help their parents. "Virtuous women," wrote a British soldier, "are selling themselves to provide food for their families."

Mention has already been made of the coal famine. During the winter of 1919–20, this was even more terrible in its results than the shortage of food. Lack of coal meant not merely a fireless grate and no cooking. It meant arrest of production, unemployment, high prices, the closing of hospitals and schools. It was closely connected with the deficiency of transport, already dislocated by the destruction and non-repair of rolling-stock, and (in certain countries) its removal by the victor states for purposes of indemnification.

The economic collapse was by no means confined to the "enemy" states. The case of Poland may be cited as an example. National bankruptcy seemed, in the autumn of 1919, to stare her in the face. More than half of her budget was allocated to military expenditure, and more than half a million of her able-bodied men were still under arms. The Ministers of Food and of Agriculture resigned in consequence of the difficulties with which they were confronted, and the lack of means at their disposal to cope with them. Food supplies from America had come to an end in July. The poorer population of the towns could get nothing for their "bread cards." In Lodz and other towns, unemployment was steadily increasing owing to the shortage of coal and raw materials. Very similar conditions prevailed over the rest of the area affected by what we have described above as "Balkanization"—the Baltic States, Roumania, the Balkan Peninsula, the Ukraine, and the Caucasus.

The financial aspect of the situation was an almost complete collapse of the credit system in the countries between the Rhine and the Volga. The failure of production, the uncertainty as to the future, the incapacity of taxation to meet even a fraction of the current Government expenditure, and (in the case of the enemy States) the mortgaging of every kind of asset to provide security for indemnities, had created a need for foreign food and raw materials which was greater than Europe had ever experienced before, but which was far beyond the power of the ordinary creators of credit to supply. The degree of the collapse could be measured by the depreciation of the currency in the various countries. Towards the end of 1919, as compared with the American dollar, the English pound had fallen over 13 per cent., the French franc 36 per cent., the Italian lira 50 per cent., the German mark 80 per cent., the Russian rouble over 90 per cent. These figures formed a more or less exact indication of the indebtedness, and the financial insecurity, of the countries concerned.

We have now pictured the economic collapse in its outward manifestations. It is necessary, however, to look closely into its causes. The important point to note is that it was no mere inevitable visitation, but was in large measure the result of a definite policy on the part of the Allied Governments.

Its origin, of course, was to be found in the economic exhaustion of the War. The immense destruction of capital values in houses, factories, mines, railways, ships, forests, and the like; the diversion of twenty millions of men from productive to unproductive labour; the blocking of the accustomed channels of international trade; these must in any case have reduced the countries concerned to poverty. But the exhaustion of the War was a cause which affected the victors as well as the vanquished; and if there had been no other, the difference between the two would have been comparatively small. "The enemy collapsed," said Mr. Hoover, the head of the American Food Administration, "not only from military and naval defeat, but from total economic exhaustion; in this race to economic chaos, the European Allies were not far behind." In point of fact, however, the difference between victor and vanquished was very great; and this was due, broadly speaking, to the policy adopted by the statesmen of the victorious countries after hostilities were over. They used their victory for the economic destruction of the beaten and crushed peoples. And the effects of such a policy could not be confined to those against whom it was primarily directed. It had its repercussions upon all the neighbouring peoples, and created a havoc which involved enemies, neutrals, and friends alike.

2. The Blockade.

Its chief instrument was the blockade of Germany, Austria, Hungary, Bulgaria, and Soviet Russia. This blockade was contrary to the opinion of the American Government, which, however, allowed itself to be overruled. Mr. Hoover energetically declared within a few weeks of the Armistice, "The blockade must be lifted." "The continuation of the blockade after the Armistice," he said in August 1919, "has destroyed enterprise even in open countries, and prevented any recovery in enemy countries." "It is my own view," he added later (September 7, 1919), "that the situation would not have been so acute if the blockade had been removed soon after the Armistice was signed, as was urged by the United States Government."

The American view was shared by many British officials. Captain Roddy, one of the fourteen British officers sent to investigate the situation in Germany at the beginning of 1919, wrote as follows: "To those who have had the opportunity of studying Germany recently from the inside, the policy of continuing the starvation of that country must appear not only senseless, but utterly harmful to ourselves."

Nevertheless the blockade was maintained, in

the strict sense of the word, against Austria for four months, and against Germany for eight months, after the fighting was over and the military power of the enemy completely broken. Against Soviet Russia and Hungary it was still in force, in practice if not in law, a whole year after the Armistice. In October 1919, Germany herself was actually invited by the Allies to join in blockading Soviet Russia—a request which she refused. States which were in no sense enemies, such as Esthonia, were also blockaded for several months.

The story of the blockade of Austria will serve to illustrate somewhat more fully the effects of the policy pursued by the Allied Governments after the Armistice.

The first convincing voice which reached the outside world as to the conditions in that country was that of Dr. Ferrière, Vice-President of the International Red Cross, who reported from Vienna in December 1918 as to the "heart-rending scenes of famine" which he had witnessed. In this gay city, one of the four or five main centres of European culture, hospitals were being closed down because the inmates had all died. Even persons operated on for cancer were being fed on cabbage. The Swiss Federal Council held a special session to consider the situation, and unanimously decided on sending relief within the measure of their power. The Swiss Minister, Dr. Bourcart, stated that as early as November 5, 1918, he had "made representations as to the impending famine in Vienna, and a memorandum containing a description of the conditions was handed to all representatives of the Entente." This, he said, was followed up by seventeen other démarches with the object of obtaining relief for the city. The President of the Swiss Federation, M. Callonder, stated that the "Federal Council has always transmitted to Paris and London the despairing messages from Vienna." Dr. Ferrière's accounts were fully confirmed by an Englishman, Colonel Summerhayes, R.A.M.C., chief of the British Mission to Prisoners of War in Austria-Hungary, who visited Vienna at this time. His verdict on the situation (December 23, 1918) was as follows: "It is his deliberate opinion as a doctor that, unless food is sent to Vienna immediately, at least 200,000 people out of a total population of 2,500,000 will die as soon as the cold weather sets in. Vienna is not on the verge of starvation, but actually starving, and people are dying like flies. During the whole of his fifteen years' medical experience in India, he says that he has never witnessed such sights as he has seen in Vienna." In January 1919, the food supplies of Austria were exhausted. Food now began to be sent in by the Allies; but the quantity was quite insufficient. "The money question is the crux," wrote the *Neue Freie Presse* (March 10th). "Paris insists on financial guarantees, but there are not sufficient. . . . If the Allies raise the blockade, and offer the merchant the chance of procuring the necessary raw materials by his credit, work will begin once more." But the blockade was maintained, and as Austria could purchase neither food nor raw materials for herself, the state of the population became terrible. Already, at the end of November, the Swiss had prepared truck-loads of food to send into the famishing city; but leave for them to pass was withheld by the Entente till a month later. After the debate in the Federal Council some train-loads were sent (early in January), but relief on this scale, as was said at the time, could only be "like a drop of water on a hot iron."

During the winter months, and up to April, the population existed mainly on cabbages and turnips; many of the poorest had literally nothing else. The milk ration, even for infants, amounted to about a teacupful, and this was supplemented by boiling down turnips to form a syrup.

Turnips were indeed the staple food, even in the hospitals, where the food consumed was about one-fifth of the normal allowance. To the misery of the turnip diet, was added that of intense cold. The hospitals could no longer be heated properly, blankets were used up, and even cold was often preferable to the pain inflicted by the hard heavy quilts pressing on the patients' emaciated limbs.

Mothers naturally suffered in a special degree. They could neither keep their children clean—for there was no soap—nor provide new clothes, nor mend the old ones—for there was no thread—nor satisfy the eternal hunger of their wasting children, even though they went hungry themselves. "If only I did not hear them crying all day long for something to eat," said a distracted mother to a member of the Swiss Relief Commission. Women would stand all night before the food shops, or in the market place, in the hope of having the first chance with the meagre supplies of turnips or possibly potatoes or apples (at 4.20 crowns per kilo) expected for sale in the morning. Many children, and grown-up people too, were too destitute of clothes to appear in the street at all, and perished slowly and unobserved in the bitter cold of their denuded homes.

Mortality was naturally appalling, and there was no wood left for coffins. Boxes were found to serve as coffins for the children (30 or 40 were dying per day in one institution holding 300); but grown-up people had to be buried in mass graves, ten bodies one over the other, with a layer of earth and lime in between. Under blockade conditions, too, no linen could be spared for grave-clothes. The dead were wrapped in paper and carried out of the town by night.

It is important to note that, during these months of unexampled horror (November 1918–March 1919), there were ample stocks of necessaries near at hand. In Switzerland (within 24 hours' journey) large stocks of substitute flour, which could no longer find sale in Switzerland, were threatening to go bad. Warehouses were congested with cotton goods, which Switzerland was not allowed to offer for sale. The blockade was strictly enforced by the Inter-Allied Commission, without whose permission nothing could be exported from Switzerland.

On February 7th, the Vienna Burgomaster, Herr Weisskirchner, speaking of the high price of United States flour, said: "I had succeeded in securing corn from the Argentine. I chartered a ship, and then it was decided that the blockade should be maintained. I prayed that exception be made for this ship, which would bring us 10,000 tons of corn. It was refused."

The blockade of Austria was raised at the end

of March 1919. But it must not be supposed that, even when blockades were technically raised, the starvation policy was abandoned. The raising of the German blockade, for example, made no difference to the terms of the Armistice, under which vast quantities of locomotives and railway trucks, of agricultural machinery, of merchant shipping, and of indispensable dock and harbour equipment, continued to be handed over. It made no difference to the terms of the Peace Treaties, whose destructive effect will be explained below. It did not release the enemy prisoners of war, who were still retained, by hundreds of thousands, in foreign camps. Nor did it imply the removal of restrictions upon trade. Embargoes and prohibitions of many kinds were still enforced.

What was more serious still, the raising of the blockade came too late. By the time it was raised, the countries affected by it had exhausted most of their resources, and had neither goods nor gold in sufficient quantity to pay for the supplies which they were now allowed, nominally, to import. The recovery which might have been possible in the first flush of relief after the Armistice, when the impetus of war-work could have been carried on into the effort of reconstruction, and the returning soldiers immediately absorbed into industry, could no longer be hoped for when the stimulus of the War had been removed, and had been succeeded by a further period of underfeeding, resentment, and uncertainty. The net result was that the distress, though slightly relieved by the raising of the blockade, remained substantially unaltered.

3. The Peace Treaties.

The blockade policy of the Allies was continued and stereotyped by the economic clauses of the Peace Treaties. The effect of these terms, many of which were of the most complicated character, was threefold. First, they deprived the enemy countries of a high proportion of the coal, raw materials, and agricultural produce on which they had formerly relied, and of ports and vital railway junctions whose loss disorganised their transport systems. Thus Germany lost the iron mines of Lorraine permanently, and the Saar coalfield for fifteen years. The fate of the Upper Silesian coalfield was, at the time of writing, still undecided. She had to hand over some forty million tons of coal a year for several years, in addition to large quantities of coal-tar, benzol, and other products. She further lost 12 per cent. of her agricultural area, which provided food for about 21 per cent. of her population.

As for Austria, she became a small community, comprising one of the greatest cities of the world and some mountain but little arable land, with no outlet to the sea. Five-sixths of her coal supply, to say nothing of the sugar-beet districts, the lead mines of Carinthia, and the oilfields of Galicia, which fed the industries of Vienna and its export trade, were handed over to the neighbouring states. Her agricultural land could only provide one-quarter of the necessary corn supplies, and less than one-quarter of the necessary potatoes.

There was another provision in the Treaties with

Germany and Austria which, from its deadly effect upon child life, and the embitterment of feeling which it left behind it, demands more than a passing reference—the enforcement of the surrender of large numbers of milch cows. Official reports established beyond question that the milk shortage in these countries was incomparably more serious that in those for whose advantage the surrender was demanded. "It is difficult to see," wrote Mr. McDougall, in the British White Paper already mentioned, "how Germany can avoid a milk famine which will endanger the lives of children and mothers to an extent we hardly dare contemplate." "Every litre of milk taken away," said Professor Starling, one of the authors of the same Report, "means a baby killed" (*Daily News, August 15th*).

These losses would not have been so serious, if political feuds had not prevented the newly-created neighbouring states from supplying German and Austrian needs by amicable arrangement. But the refusal to co-operate economically was a marked feature of the policy of these states. It was an aspect of that "Balkanization" of Europe to which allusion has been made in our second chapter. For example, the coal supplies on which Austria depended were nearly all contained in the territory of Czechoslovakia, which reduced to a minimum the export of coal to Austria. Even if such difficulties as these had been surmounted, there remained the difficulty of the foreign exchanges, which would still have compelled the distressed countries to buy, if they could buy at all, at a ruinous price.

The next effect of the Peace Treaties was the denial to the beaten states of reciprocity in commerce, and of that "equality of trade conditions among all the nations consenting to the peace" which was promised to them by the third of President Wilson's "Fourteen Points." Every facility was given to Allied subjects for trade and transport—limitation of customs tariffs, freedom from discrimination, free zones in ports, rights of residence and travel, rights to construct new railways in the territory of their former enemies. These, on the other hand, were denied all such facilities. The net result was that their hands were completely tied in the negotiating of commercial treaties, without which they could not begin to trade. Each of the states with which such negotiations took place was in a position to concede as much, or as little, as it liked. An open door being assured to it in any case, the other party had nothing to refuse, and therefore nothing to bargain with.

In the case of Germany, all her large merchant ships, half her smaller ships, and a quarter of her steam-trawlers and fishing boats had to be surrendered, while she was required to build and hand over to the Allies annually, for the next five years, 200,000 tons of new shipping. She was deprived of all her colonies, and of all concessions, treaty rights or other arrangements for the conduct of foreign trade. In view of the protectionist policy of most of the colonial powers, and the fact that her banks and business houses had been uprooted over the greater part of the world, she was threatened with total exclusion from overseas markets, whether for the purchase of food and raw materials, or for the sale of manufactured goods.

Finally, the Peace Treaties imposed an overwhelming financial burden upon the defeated countries. Germany was required to pay, by way of reparation, £5,000,000,000 "on account," and a further sum which was left wholly undetermined. These claims were a first charge—taking precedence of all domestic obligations—upon all the assets and revenues both of the Empire and of its constituent states. A "Reparation Commission" was to estimate from time to time her capacity to pay, and was, in effect, to dictate her system of internal taxation. The result was not merely to depreciate all state securities, and make financial stability impossible, but also to destroy the incentive to work on the part of the workman. The German people were told, in fact, that the harder they worked, the more they would have to pay away to the foreigner. Every working-class family was made to feel the effect of the Peace Treaty in their own persons, and in the course of their daily life. The same principles were applied to the other defeated states. In forwarding the official summary of the Austrian Peace Treaty on July 20th, the Paris correspondent of the *Times* wrote: "Faced with the pre-War debt, the War debt, a tremendous currency inflation, and the apparently overwhelming obligations imposed by the Treaty, the new Republic starts life as a bankrupt state."

4. The Human Factor.

The War, the blockade, and the Peace Treaties had not only affected men's outward surroundings, but also their ability and inclination to work. This was an aspect of war psychology which assumed great importance, during 1919, from its effect upon production. Even where all restrictions were removed, and raw materials and machinery were available, there was a marked decline in the productivity of labour, to some extent among the successful but more conspicuously among the defeated peoples. The production of Europe, according to Mr. Hoover, was "not only far below even the level of the time of the signing of the Armistice, but far below the maintenance of life and health without an unparalleled rate of import" (*National Food Journal, August* 13, 1919). "Get down to work" was the precept in which, with his sturdy American individualism, he summed up what he conceived to be the dominant need of the hour. But the problem of disinclination to work could not be isolated from the other factors in the economic collapse. "It must be evident," he said, "that production cannot increase if political incompetence continues in blockade, embargoes, censorship, mobilization, large armies, navies, and war" (Ibid.).

The sheer exhaustion of the War, and the prolonged underfeeding which followed it, was responsible for much of the slackening of effort. A traveller in the Ruhr minefield described the diet of a miner as "dry bread and substitute tea for breakfast, dry bread for dinner, and soup for supper." It was said that in Hamburg, at the docks, it took four men to do a job that had formerly been done by one. As Professor Starling said of the German workmen, in the Report already quoted, "Three years on a diet insufficient both as to quantity and quality, indigestible, tasteless, and monotonous, has not only reduced to a low level the vitality and efficiency of the great bulk of the urban population, but has also had, as might be expected, a marked influence on the mentality of the nation. Among the lower and middle classes the chief defect noted is the general apathy, listlessness, and hopelessness." Another important factor was the social ferment, itself in part, as we shall see in the next chapter, the product of distress. Different factors became prominent at different times. Now the workman would refuse to work because the product of his labour was going to the capitalist, already enriched by undue profits made out of the necessities of war; now because the same product was destined to be taken, for an indefinite time, to pay indemnities to his conquerors; now as a protest against the annexation of some particular territory by a foreign power. All these factors were rendered more serious by the physical conditions under which the work had to be done. The underfeeding and nerve-exhaustion intensified the discontent, the irritability, the bitterness, the despair; these sapped the will to work, and lowered production; the lowered production, in its turn, aggravated the underfeeding, and thus the vicious circle began anew.

5. The Great Refusal.

It is evident, from what has been said, that the economic collapse was very far from being inevitable. Many of its evils might have been prevented if the blockade policy had been abandoned, and still more if a positive scheme of economic assistance had been adopted.

As a matter of fact, certain steps were taken in this direction by the various bodies which had been formed during the War to co-ordinate the economic resources of the Allies. The logic of the Allied policy was tempered by a certain kindly inconsistency, due to the presence in the official world of many men to whom it was wholly repugnant. A "Consultative Food Committee" was set up to advise the "Reparation Commission." The Supreme Economic Council, which carried out the blockade against Germany and Austria, was at the same time sending Relief Missions to certain distressed areas, notably to Vienna. Mr. Hoover established a great organization for the feeding of school-children. The American Congress voted a large sum for the relief of Allied and neutral countries in Europe. Great Britain advanced some £12,000,000, largely to Austria. Many of the Allied officials, both civil and military, faced with the human realities of the situation, made a brave attempt to mitigate its horrors. They took advantage of every opportunity, and stretched the limits of their competence to the utmost, in order to avert the worst disasters of starvation, disease, and industrial disorganization.

But the general policy of the Allies remained

unaltered. It was indeed a questionable kindness to give temporary relief in the worst cases of distress, while at the same time preventing the resumption of trade and industry, and refusing the wider measures of economic reconstruction, such as the raw materials and the transport facilities, which would have enabled the people concerned to rebuild their industrial life for themselves, and so rendered the relief unnecessary.

A considerable amount of economic co-operation had been established among the Allies during the War. It consisted of two parts—a negative and a positive. They co-operated both for the economic destruction of the enemy, and for the pooling of their own resources according to the degree of need. Broadly speaking, the policy now pursued was to maintain the negative part and to drop the positive. The destructive measures have been described above. The positive co-operation, on the other hand, which might have been extended so as to effect a pooling of the world's resources in the interest of all nations, was abandoned. No definite international policy was adopted. The co-ordination of the supply of shipping, raw materials, coal and food was allowed to lapse in favour of private enterprise. Distribution according to need was replaced by distribution according to immediate ability to pay. The short-term interests of private capital were preferred to the long-term interests of peoples. No measures of any magnitude were taken to supply the credit without which the crushed peoples were unable to purchase what they needed; nor were any steps taken to reconsider the destructive clauses of the Peace Treaties, in the light of the need of world-reconstruction, now so clearly revealed.

The principle of "rationing"—the principle that "no one should have cake until all have bread," as it was expressed by the British Labour Party—had proved its value during the War, both in the internal economy of each state, and in the utilization of the common resources of several states. Had it been retained in both of these spheres, it would have gone far to remedy the shortage which now prevailed. It would have restricted the consumption of luxuries which now began again, in almost every country, on the part of the fortunate individuals who could afford to pay for them. This restriction in each country would have left a larger surplus of necessaries for export to other countries. But this was too great a sacrifice, alike for the more fortunate states, and for the more fortunate individuals within each state. The rationing system was relaxed, both in its national and in its international forms. Milk, for instance, was consumed as cream which, in a condensed form, might have saved the lives of thousands of children in distant lands. Nor were the needs of the distressed populations allowed to stand in the way of unproductive war-expenditure. Soldiers were kept under arms by millions, and prisoners of war confined in camps by hundreds of thousands, who might have been producing the necessaries of life. Supplies were sent to Admiral Kolchak and General Denikin which might have fed starving towns.

6. Starvation as a Weapon.

Nor was it only that the more fortunately placed countries refused to husband their resources for the production of necessaries, or to share their food, money, and materials with those in desperate need. They were, owing to their more favoured economic position, enabled to exercise a power over the rest of the world which they were not slow to use for political purposes. The Allied Governments controlled nearly all the exportable surpluses of food, coal, and raw materials, and nearly all the means of transport. They could dictate their policy by starvation—or even by the mere threat of starvation—far more effectively than by military or naval force. They held in their hands a weapon which no conqueror of former times, from Alexander to Napoleon, had ever wielded; and they employed it upon a scale unprecedented in history. It was by the use of this weapon that Germany was forced to sign a Treaty which violated the Agreement upon which she had laid down her arms; and the threat of it was used on later occasions to enforce the execution of particular terms in the Treaty. The most frequent use of the economic weapon, however, was in connexion with the struggle against the spread of Socialism. The blockade of Soviet Russia and Soviet Hungary has been already described. But these were only two examples among many. The threat to withhold essential supplies was used—such at any rate was the general belief—to cause the retirement of the Socialist Government of Moraczevski in Poland, and to prevent the creation of a Socialist Government in Lettland. It was used against the border states of the former Russian Empire, to induce them to continue the war against the Bolshevists. Where a moderate Socialist Government existed, it was used to prevent the rise of a Communist Government to power.

On April 12, 1919, the Vienna Government was informed by the Allies that the food supply would be at once stopped in the event of riots, or (as another of the Allied authorities put it) "of a Communist or Bolshevist rising." The leading daily paper (*Neue Freie Presse*) impressed its readers with the fact that Vienna had not even two days' supplies of food, and the Entente would not hesitate "to use the death penalty" if their behests were not observed. The British Military Representative repeated later on that "The British Government stands by its declaration of April 12th, that in the event of disorders in Austria, the import of food and raw materials would immediately be stopped" (*Morning Post, June 25th*). The Social-Democratic leaders made constant efforts to hold back the people from a Communist revolution, never ceasing to represent to them that it would mean the withdrawal of Entente supplies. "My lunch consists of lentil soup," wrote an American correspondent, "followed by American pork. . . . It is not very nice; but it is a very wonderful two ounces of meat, for it alone prevented Vienna from going Bolshevist any time this last fortnight. I mean it represents one man's share of the twelve Entente food trains which are daily coming into Vienna. Without it Vienna would starve to death in a week; and Vienna knows it, and knows that the Entente would stop the food trains if Vienna turned Bolshevist" (*New York Times, May* 8, 1919).

7. The Doom of the Surplus Population.

The saner heads among the Allied statesmen began to realize, in the latter half of 1919, that the policy of destruction had been a disastrous mistake. But by that time it had been pushed to such extremes that nothing short of a long and costly process of "nursing back to life" could have undone its effects. At the close of the year the best judges predicted that the under-production of Central and Eastern Europe, and consequently the high prices which affected all countries alike, must necessarily continue for a long period unless recuperative measures, of which there was as yet no sign, were immediately taken. Mr. McCurdy, Parliamentary Secretary to the British Food Ministry, stated in October 1919: "So long as the industrial life of Central and Eastern Europe remains in its present state of paralysis there is no prospect of any general fall in prices." Mr. Hoover declared that "the productivity of Europe to-day is such that Europe could not survive twelve months"; that "Europe, and the world, is actually in the presence of the greatest danger which has overtaken mankind." Sir George Paish (*Ways and Means, November* 18, 1919) said that "As matters now stand, with no comprehensive plan for inducing the world to pool its supplies and its credits, the outlook is that Europe in the spring of next year will be subjected to famine conditions and that even more life will be sacrificed than was destroyed in the War itself."

To put the matter in a nutshell, a large part of Europe was now condemned to economic conditions which rendered it impossible to support the existing population. That population, before the War, was at least 100,000,000 in excess of what could have been supported without trade with the outside world. These great numbers could only live by producing vast quantities of goods for export, and rendering various services to countries outside Europe, in exchange for raw materials and other necessaries. This was the case, in particular, according to Mr. Hoover, with no less than 25 or 30 millions of Germans and Austrians. The new conditions rendered impossible the continuance of this exchange on anything like the same scale. The old distribution of productive and commercial energy throughout the world—a distribution due, in large measure, to the relative suitability of the various countries and races for the parts they had to play—had been violently altered, from motives of political domination or one-sided economic aggrandisement. Russia was, for some time at any rate, practically eliminated from the world's economic system, both as a market and as a source of supplies. The basis of German and Austrian industry, as it had existed before the War, was cut away. One of the strangest anomalies was the relative situation of Germany and France. France, with a people diminishing in numbers and mainly non-industrial in character, was in possession of territories capable of supporting an immensely larger population. Germany, with a much more numerous people, was confined to a smaller territory, deprived of essential raw materials, and shut out from colonial trade.

There were only two conceivable ways by which an economic equilibrium could be restored. One way would have been the complete alteration of the new conditions, either by voluntary renunciation on the part of the conquerors, or by a series of new wars for the reconquest of territory and the securing of commercial rights and openings both within and outside Europe. Any such alteration, in the circumstances, was plainly impossible. There remained the other alternative—that of adaptation to the new conditions; or in other words, the reduction of the populations concerned to the smaller number which it was now possible to maintain. Speaking of Germany, Mr. Hoover gave it as his opinion that "one possibility that must not be overlooked is that 10 or 12 millions of this population may emigrate Eastward or overseas, under the economic pressure which will be their fate at the best." The German official estimate was 15 millions. Professor Starling wrote (Cmd. 280) that the country under the new conditions was over-populated, "and it seems probable that within the next few years many million . . . workers and their families will be obliged to emigrate, since there will be neither work nor food for them to be obtained from the reduced industries of the country." As to Austria, an eminent Allied authority predicted that within two or three years "half the population must emigrate or be killed off."

Such a process was bound to have a disastrous

influence upon the general standard of living. The competition of starving and desperate workmen for employment, whether in their own country or elsewhere, was destined to be a serious impediment in the way of raising the conditions of labour throughout the world. The German and Austrian working-class was confronted with the further difficulty that many of the principal industrial countries were closed to them by the anti-alien legislation which was maintained in force after the War. But even had these countries been open to them, the reduction of their population must needs be accompanied by an incalculable amount of human suffering. "Economic pressure," strong enough to drive 10 or 12 millions of people from their homes, implies conditions of unemployment, destitution, and disease which would cause the death, in all probability, of as many millions as would finally succeed in emigrating. The story of the great Irish famine of 1847 is the classical example of the process. A sordid scramble for existence, indefinitely prolonged, would be the lot of those who remained behind. In the light of such a prospect, men began to recall the horrors of the Thirty Years' War, when the population of the Empire was reduced by 10 millions, although only 350,000 had fallen in battle. "Famine, disease, and emigration," says the historian, "had done the rest."

CHAPTER V

THE MEANING OF BOLSHEVISM

Remotâ justitiâ, quid regna nisi magna latrocinia?
St. Augustine.

1. The Supreme Issue.

We have seen that one element in the collapse of Europe was the turmoil produced by the new social upheaval. The magnitude of this upheaval, and the difficulty of obtaining accurate information, render an adequate account of it almost impossible. Yet one thing is certain, that in it is involved the supreme issue of the hour—something of far greater human significance than the question of crushing Germany, or setting up new national states. The whole social foundation upon which modern industrial states have been built up is now definitely called in question; and this not by a few thinkers and agitators, but by actual social transformations, or attempted transformations. The wide ramifications of the movement, whether in its successful or its embryonic forms, have been fully described in our third chapter.

In treating all these ramifications as parts of one great movement, we do not ignore the fact that the coming of Socialism to power in one state after another gave rise to a conflict, of an intensity hitherto unknown, within the ranks of Socialism itself. Unity was not difficult so long as the main function of Socialism was that of protest. But when a particular section of Socialists, whether Communist or Social Democratic—a term which at this time became identified with the more moderate type of Socialism—came into actual power, a new set of problems appeared on the horizon. The party in power had to administer the country, to maintain order, and to keep itself in office while doing so. It found itself compelled to use the methods, or some of them, which all Governments have used for these purposes. Which of these methods ought to be used, whether they ought to be used against Socialist opponents, and in particular how far it is legitimate for Socialists to employ military force, censorship, and the control of the press, became burning issues. These violent antagonisms, however, do not alter the fact that, at bottom, all the great social changes now taking place have been inspired by the same idea. The historian will treat them as different aspects of one movement, just as, in the break-up which followed the Reformation, he traces the controversy of Lutherans and Calvinists as an incident in a greater struggle—the Protestant Revolution.

The struggle within the ranks of Socialism reached its highest point of intensity in Germany. The "Majority Socialists," who held the principal Government posts, declared that the desperate state of the country, following upon the Peace Treaty, made it absolutely necessary that order should be maintained, if the people were not to starve to death, or freeze to death, and if the ruin were not to become wholly irreparable. They accused the "Independent Socialists" of stirring up agitation with a reckless disregard of this elementary necessity, and of playing into the hands of the Communists for the sake of popularity, while refusing to share the responsibility of government. The Independent Socialists in their turn denounced the Government as anti-Socialist, as relying upon the same militarist forces as the Kaiser had done, and as being the main pillar of the "bourgeois" reaction. They claimed to be distinguished from the Communists by the fact that they acted upon a preconceived plan of campaign, rather than upon a policy of sporadic and unorganized street fighting. They drew, however, nearer and nearer to the general Communist position, and refused to condemn those movements of armed resistance to the Government which broke out from time to time in Berlin, Hamburg, Bremen, Dusseldorf, Halle, and other industrial towns. The most tragic of these conflicts was that which, in the beginning of 1919, brought into power the transient Communist Government of Munich. The Bavarian capital, associated in most minds with love of art, spotless cleanliness, and a peculiar geniality of character, became for a time a scene of ferocity on both sides, which the terrible psychological effects of suffering and despair can alone explain.

2. The Communist Theory.

The form which the Revolution took in Russia is that which is best worth studying. It was in Moscow that the new idea first clothed itself in a practical form so striking as to rivet the attention of the whole world; and the chief interest of

European politics centred round that burning focus of activity, as it had centred round Paris in 1789. Further, the Russian Revolution illustrates with great vividness the most characteristic features of the new movement. At the same time, we must be careful not to regard such extreme forms as a necessary and inevitable part of the social transformation. Russian conditions, as we shall see below, are in many respects unique.

The Russian Communist starts from the belief that the present state of society is a dictatorship. The dictators are that minority of the people who own property in considerable quantities. This minority not only controls our economic and political life, both in home and foreign affairs; what is much more important is that it controls our minds, particularly through education and the press. It has entrenched itself so firmly that, though only a small minority, it has secured the acquiescence of the main mass of the people in its domination, and the domination of its ideas.

To overthrow this domination is the aim of the class struggle. This struggle is more important than any possible struggle between nations. If we really want to bring about a change in society which will put down the mighty from their seat and exalt them of low degree, we can only do it by carrying out, in the interest of the non-propertied, the same process that the propertied have carried out in their own interest—only in the reverse direction.

In this reverse process—which is the Social Revolution—the initial steps must be taken by a minority acting on behalf of the non-propertied.

So long as the propertied minority has all the reins in its hands, it is futile to expect that you can convert the majority of the people at once to the new view of things. Universal suffrage and parliamentary democracy, under the present circumstances, will merely register the acquiescence of the mass in the existing condition of society.

A minority—an "advanced guard," as Lenin calls it—consisting of those who are conscious of the true state of affairs, and prepared to act in the interest of the non-propertied, must take control of the Government. This minority will, in practice, be found among the industrial workers. It must immediately set to work to destroy the privileges of property. Food, houses, manufacture, education, entertainment, must all be controlled in such a way as to give as much of the good things of life to the poor as to the rich.

The new economic system must be built up gradually, by laborious and self-sacrificing work. Institutions (e.g. Soviets) must be established which will enable the interests and point of view of the non-propertied to be expressed, to the exclusion of those of the propertied. This is the distinguishing feature of the Soviet system as it exists in Russia. Though generally regarded as a necessary part of the Communist doctrine, it is not so in reality. The war-cry of "All power to the Soviets" was only adopted in Russia after the Communists had obtained a majority in those bodies. It is evident that the mere grouping of electors according to their occupation, instead of according to their place of residence, would not necessarily yield a revolutionary result. The

German Soviets have shown a much more conservative character than the Russian, and this tendency would probably be more pronounced in countries further West.

The minority thus placed in power—the Communist would continue—will rapidly secure the support of the majority of the non-propertied. From that moment the true "dictatorship of the proletariat" begins.

But it is not enough to build up the new social system. You must root out the old. Resolute war must be waged against the efforts that will be made to overthrow the Government.

These efforts will be immense, for the propertied class has its roots and its tentacles everywhere; its hangers-on are innumerable; and it will be supported by foreign bayonets. This last fact makes it imperatively necessary to appeal to the proletariat of other countries to take control of their Governments.

As and when the propertied class realizes that the new régime has come to stay, it will gradually come over to that régime. This process must be hastened by penalizing those who do not, in comparison with those who do. The "bourgeois" will gradually become workers in the service of the new régime. It is by this means that the "bourgeoisie" will be eliminated. Then will come into existence "the Communist order, where there will be no hatred of one class against another, because there will be no classes at all."[1]

But, until this state of affairs arrives, there must be a stage of transition. It is at this point that

[1] Trotsky: *The Soviet Power and International Imperialism*, p. 5.

the controversy begins which has divided so sharply the "Right" and the "Left" elements in the Socialist International. Problems of extraordinary difficulty, both theoretical and practical, at once come into view. How long may this stage be legitimately prolonged? It is not disputed that, for a brief revolutionary moment, the methods of war may be adopted by the party which seizes power. But are they justified in incorporating these methods of war into their system of administration, and continuing to apply them for months or even for years? The answer of the Russian Communist is clear. This stage of transition must be continued as long as it is necessary. It is essentially a stage of civil war, though it need not be carried on by methods of violence. The methods adopted must be judged by the standards which we apply to civil war, not those we apply to normal civil life. Every Government suppresses rebellion against itself, and a Communist Government must do it as much as any other. Hence the fight against "counter-Revolution."

The Communist Government must refuse to give its opponents any share in political power. Hence it cannot accept—during the transition—a Constituent Assembly chosen by universal suffrage.

It must keep in its own hands the machinery by which public opinion is formed—press, schools, and all methods of propaganda—and use that machinery for forming anew the whole mind of the nation. Hence it cannot accept—during the transition—liberty of the press, of meeting, or of instruction.

This process must be clearly recognized as one

of transition only. The ultimate goal is a state in which the new form of Government will be generally acquiesced in; and then complete democracy will be possible. But, on the other hand, the process cannot be a short one. It can only come to an end when "the working class has got its enemies firmly in hand—has knocked the pride out of the propertied class—and the propertied class has given up all hope of ever coming to power again." [1]

There is nothing in this theory which had not been previously discussed by Socialists. The conception of a class conflict, far transcending all national conflicts in importance, and the methods of resolving that conflict, have been a commonplace of debate for half a century, at least among the Continental parties. Russian Communism, at bottom, is Marxian Socialism, with the same sharply defined historical background, and the same materialist basis in philosophy. What is new in it is the rigid logic with which it applies familiar ideas. The average Continental Socialist of the rank and file, if asked to give in a word its chief characteristic, would probably single out its "irreconcilability" (*Unversöhnlichkeit*) as opposed to the conciliatory character of the theories previously prevailing. It differs, again, from earlier statements of Socialist theory, because it has been forced to take account of a whole crop of practical problems never seriously faced before. Typical of these are the questions of Sovietism *versus* Parliamentarism; of the methods by which property should be expropriated; and of the principle on which a force should be created for the armed defence of the Revolution.

[1] Bucharin: *The Programme of the Communists*, p. 21.

3. The Effects of the War.

Such is the Communist theory as it appears in the writings of its Russian exponents. But it cannot be usefully discussed apart from the environment in which it first became a great European force. No doubt, even without the War, it would in time have taken practical shape. But the embodiment would probably have come at a different time and in a different form, upon which it is useless to speculate. As a matter of history, it was the War that brought the Communist movement to power, and stamped a particular character both upon its theory and upon its practice. In studying the effects of the War upon it, we shall learn to distinguish between what is temporary and local in it, and what is general and essential.

We must note, first, that the movement was to some extent one of desperation. It cannot be understood, unless we first realize the collapse of Europe which has been described in previous chapters, and the deep psychological effects produced by the long agony of the War. The theory of some Socialists, that social conditions must become worse in order to become better, seemed confirmed by the events of the time. The movement arose, as was natural, in the defeated countries. Their peoples seemed to have nothing more to lose. They were experiencing a misery so unprecedented that the possible miseries of the future had little terror for them. Despair and cynicism had destroyed all restraining influences. The victorious peoples had transient but real satisfactions which, for the time at least, made them comparatively impervious to the new idea. It was only in proportion as their common interest with the rest of humanity was driven painfully home by high prices and industrial stagnation, that they too became accessible to the new, disintegrating force.

But the War had done something more than produce suffering and chaos. It had produced a general belief in violence. Violent methods had been seen operating on such a gigantic scale, that all others seemed remote and shadowy by comparison. Hence the exaggerated emphasis which is placed in the Communist theory upon force. Again and again in the writings of Lenin, of Trotsky, and of Bucharin, the idea recurs that the possession of the power of the state, the wielding of the administrative machine, is the supreme goal. There are no half-lights in the picture, no degrees in the scale. There are simply two sharply distinct classes contending for one perfectly definite and indivisible weapon—namely, power.

The War had taught another lesson which was not lost upon the partizans of Communism. Sudden and dramatic reversals of fortune had come to seem normal and natural. It was perhaps to be expected that such an idea should take root in Russia, where military advances and retreats had taken place on an unparalleled scale. The Russian Armies, after having invaded East Prussia in the first weeks of the War, had been subsequently driven for hundreds of miles without a pause, through a line of great fortresses, Grodno, Kovno, Vilna, Dvinsk, to within gunshot of Petrograd. On the other hand the Germans, within the short space of eight months, had been dashed down from the pinnacle of power upon which they had stood at Brest-Litovsk (March 3, 1918) to the humiliation of the Armistice (November 11, 1918). World-shaking military events such as these could not fail to influence men's minds. Evolutionism, in all its forms, was discredited. The belief in mass movements made upon impulse, without clearly defined aims—strikes for the sake of striking, the "politics of the street," all that is implied in the slang word "Putschism"—intruded itself into the highly rationalized system of Russian Communism, to which it is in reality so alien. Men were led to expect some vast and sweeping social change, some world-revolution. In the eyes of the simpler devotees it took on the lurid colours of an apocalyptic vision, in which the sheep and the goats would be dramatically divided.

There is another cause which gave to Russian Communism its extreme character. This was the disillusionment which followed the failure of the "Liberal" professions of the statesmen. These empty phrases, it was said, were the best which "Bourgeois Democracy" could produce. Here was a state of society which could proclaim the "Fourteen Points" as its goal, and then tear them up like any scrap of paper. It was with such a society, not with any imaginary or ideal system of government, that the Socialist conception was contrasted. Socialists made full use of the exposure of "Liberal ideals" which the War had brought in its train.

Nor was it the Liberals alone, in the stricter sense of the word, who were discredited. Those

Socialists who, in pursuance of the "sacred union" for national defence, had supported their Governments during the war, had patently failed to produce the least effect upon Government policy. It so happened that these Socialists had generally been those who belonged to the Revisionist school. This was conspicuously so in Germany, with one remarkable exception, that of Edward Bernstein. The men who had adhered most uncompromisingly to Marxist principles, were also the men who had fought against their Governments and braved the storm of popular hatred. It was the Marxists, not the Revisionists, who had gathered together at Zimmerwald and Kienthal an "International" which, however small and feeble it might have been, had held consistently aloft the flag of Internationalism. Hence the credit attaching to them and to their views after the War was over, after the "sacred union" had become a thing of the past, and its supporters had begun to discover how deeply they had been deceived in its name.

4. Local Differences.

Such were the temporary causes which left their mark on the Russian Communist movement during the year following the War, and in a greater or less degree upon the whole Socialist movement of the time. But wide divergencies were also created by differences in local conditions. It is of special importance to realize this point in the case of Russia. In that country the capitalist class is very small in numbers, and is clearly marked off from the rest of the people. The "proletariat" (if in that term we include the families who cultivate a minute number of acres by their own labour) forms the overwhelming mass of the population. Again, the vast size of the country makes it difficult to maintain control from the centre, and therefore to secure a Civil Service which will not include a great proportion of impostors, self-seekers, and bullies. Another feature of the country, which has left its mark upon the Communist as upon other parties, is the atmosphere of bitter theoretical controversy which has always prevailed there. This has been especially the case amongst Socialists, who were excluded under the old régime from all share in practical politics. Absorbed in discussion, they were led to magnify their differences to the utmost, whilst at the same time they developed a keenness and precision of thought which accounts for the logical rigour of their doctrine. Lenin, Trotsky, Bucharin, must be seen against this background in order to be understood.

The conditions in Hungary were different. The Communist Government which held power from March to August 1919, succeeded in carrying through the social transformation with far less violence than the Russians. Their leader, Bela Kun, had spent months in Russia in the study of Communist methods, with the deliberate aim of learning how to avoid the mistakes which had been made in that country. Until the last weeks of turmoil and internal strife, which preceded the overthrow of his Government by the Allies, there were few, if any, executions. Within the Government itself, the Moderates held their own throughout, Kunfi, who had taken part in the "Second" International at Berne, maintaining the view that the suppression of opinion was neither justifiable nor necessary.

How largely the nature of the movement is affected by local conditions is shown by the widely varying forms which it assumes. In countries where the population is mainly agricultural, such as the Ukraine, the Baltic Provinces, Georgia, and Armenia, Socialism means little more than the socialization of a very few large industries, and the dividing up of Crown lands, Church lands, and feudal estates among the peasantry. In Germany, and to a certain degree in Austria, the problem is that of taking over a vast, well-established, and complicated industrial machine. Here it has so far proved impossible to effect the transformation at once. The fulfilment seems always to lag behind the promise. Distinctions are drawn between the industries which are ripe for socialization, and those which are not. In the social transformations that are destined to follow further West, the divergences from the Russian model will be greater still.

This variety of manifestation explains, among other things, the differences which have divided the Socialist movement itself. These are due, not so much to inherently irreconcilable views as to the temporary and local conditions under which it has to operate.

5. The Pros and Cons.

To sum up the rights and wrongs of the Russian Communist movement would be impossible. The observer can do little more at present than take note of all the indications as yet available, clear his mind of prejudices, and render himself immune from the deliberate conspiracies of deception which assail him from opposite sides. Any judgment as to details must be provisional. It is hard to ascertain the facts. Doubtless they vary immensely in different districts of Russia, and this explains in part the wide discrepancies in the accounts given.

The movement is being tried, again, under unprecedented and unnatural conditions. It is easy to point out its shortcomings. But how many of these are due to the menace of foreign invasion? How much to political uncertainty as to the allocation of territory? How much to the economic exhaustion which had already revealed itself before any of the Revolutions began at all? Take, for instance, the lowering of productivity which has undoubtedly taken place, and which is so often attributed to the spread of Socialism and Communism. The fact is that it would have occurred in any case, owing to the physical, psychological, and economic collapse produced by the War. It can easily be accounted for, quite apart from the effects of social disturbance. To what extent is it really aggravated by these new influences? The attempt to prove that it is entirely due to them must be examined with suspicion; for it is at the present moment the supreme interest of the possessing classes to spread abroad the idea that decreased productivity is caused by the revolutionary spirit, or in other words, that it could be remedied by a contented acquiescence in the capitalist system.

There is in these matters a vicious circle. Economic collapse leads to political revolution. Political revolution, in its turn, intensifies economic collapse. It cannot be otherwise. The transformation at which the revolutionary movement aims could only be carried out successfully and smoothly if it were effected with the utmost care, if the best minds were concentrated upon it at leisure, if experiments could freely be made, and statistics were readily available. But as things are, this delicate operation has to be carried out by rough and ready methods, under conditions almost of chaos, and often in the midst of civil war. Nor must we forget the power, which the capitalist system inherently possesses, of preventing the substitution of any other system for itself. Good or bad, it holds the field; such production as goes on is in its hands; if it cannot do anything else, it can at least stop this production, or threaten to stop it—a form of "sabotage" which is destined to play a sinister part in the changes of the near future. The new system, on the other hand, cannot be created in a sufficiently short space of time to keep the machinery running, and avoid the fatal break.

The difficult circumstances in which the new social movement has to operate have been naturally used, by those responsible for leading it, as an excuse for desperate measures. The Communist régime and the Social-Democratic régime alike are haunted by the fears of "Counter-Revolution." The unseen enemy in your midst (as we know from our own experience of spy-fever) is more alarming even than the enemy at the gate. The fear of these "dark forces" occasionally rises to panic, and a "Red Terror" follows. Can necessity be pleaded for such excesses? Some say that it can; they argue that the Hungarian Communists were overthrown for the very reason that they adopted milder methods than the Russian, and had failed to strike terror to the heart of the "Counter-Revolutionaries" in their midst. It is easy to point out that the terror of the "Reds" is generally outdone by the terror of the "Whites"; that the proscriptions and persecutions of the Russian Revolution have never approached in magnitude those of the Tsar; that atrocities occur in all revolutions; that they are largely caused by foreign military intervention, which keeps alive the flames of civil war. Such arguments fail to convince, because they do not touch the root of the question. What is perhaps more to the point is to note that the evidence cited in support of "atrocities" is generally the evidence of witnesses who cannot be unprejudiced—men dispossessed of their property by the new régime, exiles long absent, bitter party opponents, and émigrés driven from their homes.

The case against the Communists does not really rest upon "atrocities," though, for reasons which are sufficiently obvious, the statesmen and the press have moved heaven and earth to shift it on to that ground. It rests, in reality, upon the way in which they have pressed the conception of civil war to its extreme consequences. They have used the starvation weapon, exactly as the Allied statesmen have used it, against those whom they wished to penalize. In placing the property owner, or the employer of another man's labour, in the lowest category as regards rations, their object is, of course, not primarily to starve these classes, but to force them to become the direct servants of the state. But since it is quite impossible that the state service could immediately absorb the whole of these classes, the actual effect is merely to force them, through physical suffering, into a general subservience to the Government of the day. Many concessions are made in practice to ease the transition, but on the other hand the system is clearly open to all manner of abuse.

The disfranchisement of the propertied classes, including the dissolution of the Constituent Assembly on the precise ground that it rested on the votes of all classes, is only the most obvious application of a principle which, however much justified in theory in a period of revolutionary transition, is fraught with infinite danger if it is maintained over a long period. The actual degree in which the Communists have suppressed the freedom of the press, of meeting, of teaching, and of propaganda generally, is still a matter of controversy. But the actual facts are of the less importance in this case, because the serious charge is that the suppression of thought and opinion is defended by the theorists of Communism, and defended with a force and energy which recalls the most outspoken champions of autocracy. No supporter of Government policy in the belligerent countries has a right to criticize the Communists in this respect, if once he concedes that they are engaged in a struggle of vital importance. But they may well be criticized by those who are jealous of the maintenance of freedom, even at the cost of some risk to immediate success in the struggle. These may well ask whether there are not wider interests than those of the moment; whether the creation of a tyrannical tradition of government, with its consequent embitterment and the certainty of appalling reprisals, are not too heavy a price to pay for the realization of any immediate political aim; whether criticism, and especially the criticism of fellow-Socialists who believe in attaining the same aim by other methods, does not provide the indispensable security for correcting mistakes of judgment on the part of the minority in power.

On the other hand, the Communists can claim that, though the process has certainly been accompanied by widespread suffering and injustice to individuals, nevertheless the social transformation has been, for the first time in history, achieved. This fact, and not Bolshevist propaganda, constitutes the real power of Lenin over men's minds. Those who would fight Bolshevism to-day must fight it by achieving its aims without committing its blunders or crimes. In Russia, and for a space in Hungary, the poor man has been given as much food as the rich. He has had an equal opportunity of entertainment and artistic pleasure. Extraordinary strides have been made in popular education. Prostitution has been largely eliminated from Moscow. The poor man's children, equally with those of the rich, have been treated with exceptional solicitude and care. The prohibition of alcohol has been rigidly enforced. Housing accommodation has been equally shared. The men who have actually grappled, however roughly, with the appalling housing problem of Buda-Pesth or Moscow, may well retort to their critics, "You can show that we have done it badly, but can you show that you ever attempted to do it at all?"

In the great questions of the land, and of the administration of industry, the Communists have compromised. Their theoretic scheme of large-scale co-operative agriculture has foundered upon the rock of peasant prejudice. The individualism of the peasant is undoubtedly the most fundamental obstacle to socialization throughout Europe. The Communists have, broadly speaking, confirmed the handing over of the great estates to small individual ownership, which was the old policy of the Social Revolutionary Party, and was passed by the Constituent Assembly under the leadership of Chernov. In industry, the control of works and factories by the workmen employed in them, which was open to the charge of "setting up new capitalists in place of the old," has been replaced by a system in which the wider interests of trade unions and localities find representation. Technical experts are paid at the rate which their services could command in a competitive market. At least it may be said that valuable experiments are being made; and it is surely unfair to attack the Communists, first for their extreme proposals, and then for not carrying them out.

On its international side, the theory of Communism is that of all convinced Socialists. The essential division of humanity is regarded as a horizontal, not a vertical one; the conflict of interest between the possessing and non-possessing classes as of greater human moment than any struggle between nations. The main feature of Communist diplomacy has been its consistent appeal to the peoples of all countries, and its relative indifference to their Governments.

By its publication of the secret archives of the Russian Foreign Office, the Soviet Government has struck a blow, destined perhaps to be a mortal one, at the whole fabric of secret diplomacy. Its action in making peace with Germany, when Kerensky had failed to do so for six months, formed the most notable point of difference between the Revolution of November and the Revolution of March. It was significant of the Communists' rigour in the application of principles. The Brest-Litovsk negotiations—the whole story of the unanswered appeal to the conscience and the interests of the world-proletariat—still remain a monument of democratic diplomacy, whose idealism goes far to redeem its tragic failure.

6. The End of an Epoch.

We seem to have travelled far from our starting-point in "high politics," when we find ourselves discussing the housing of Russian or Hungarian artizans. Yet this is merely a true reflection of the change in values which the new age has brought in its train. These questions, with their international implications, are in fact the point around which the real conflicts of the immediate future are destined to rage.

The change by which social problems have superseded national problems as the primary subject of interest and of conflict, is so gigantic as to justify us in regarding the crisis, through which we are now passing, as the end of an epoch. It is not the first of such great transitions. In the march of history, it may be placed side by side with the breakdown of the idea of religious privilege which culminated in the Thirty Years' War; or with the breakdown of the idea of political privilege, the declaration of the Rights of Man, and the assertion of individual political freedom, which opened the floodgates of the Napoleonic Wars. It is not without significance that in each case the breakdown was accompanied by years of war and conflict. In each case, an idea was challenged which had served as a main prop to the structure of civilization then existing; and the result was a falling in of that structure at many points apparently unconnected with the prop itself. The Thirty Years' War, says the historian, "absorbed all the local wars of Europe." In each case, all the riotous forces which had long been held in check or in equilibrium were let loose. And in each case, to those whose interests had been bound up with the old order, the change seemed nothing but a general collapse, an unintelligible chaos, the end of all things. Even to the great mass who live from hand to mouth, whose thoughts never travel outside their family or their village, except when disturbed at long intervals by some vague war-cry from the unknown outer world, even to these the old order to which they had become accustomed seemed, in its orderliness, to be tolerable and even beautiful, when compared with the plunge into the unknown which they were now invited to take.

We appear to be witnessing to-day another such

transformation, in which the whole idea of social privilege is in course of being broken down. If this analysis be correct, things will not right themselves automatically, nor will the destined readjustments be reached in a short period of time. We are faced with a prolonged period of conflict, from which no industrial country, at any rate, can remain exempt. At the beginning of such a period, men are tempted to believe that the new idea, which clashes with their accepted habits of thought, must be fought and destroyed at all costs. The ruling classes could see nothing in the French Revolution except "Jacobinism," and it seemed to them justifiable to inflict untold misery upon the populations of Europe in order to eradicate that terrible germ. Those who are fighting against the new idea to-day are incurring the same responsibility as those who then plunged Europe into twenty-two years of war, who caused the rise of Napoleon, and yet failed after all to suppress the revolutionary principle. The least that we in our generation can do is to give to the new movement a full and free opportunity of growth and experiment. On no other terms can we hope to appear with clean hands at the bar of history.

CHAPTER VI

WHOM THE GODS WOULD DESTROY

Quem deus vult perdere, prius dementat.

Ancient Proverb.

1. The Blindness of the Statesmen.

We have now completed, in broad outlines, the picture of the world-situation during the year following the Armistice. In this chapter we shall discuss the part which the Allied statesmen have played in creating that situation.

In speaking of the Allied statesmen alone, we make it clear that we are not dealing with the responsibility for the outbreak of the War. For this the enemy statesmen bear their full share. We are speaking of its prolongation, the settlement of its issues, and the treatment of the conditions which it left behind it.

The responsibility of the Allied statesmen is not, of course, without limits. We know the difficulties they had to face. Some of them made efforts to apply the principles they had proclaimed, and were resisted by others. We realize that the statesmen are sometimes the slaves of circumstance. It is easy to see, in particular, how one betrayal of principle inevitably leads on to another.

We know, too, how hard it is to ascertain what was passing behind the closed doors. Great importance must be attached, in this connexion, to the evidence of the half-dozen men who, at one time or another, deliberately violated official reticence, and took the risk of telling the public what they knew—men such as Mr. Douglas Young, Colonel Sherwood-Kelly, Mr. John Maynard Keynes, Mr. Bullitt in America, and a few others. These men have shed some gleams, at least, upon the dark passages of secret diplomacy.

Nor must the responsibility of the peoples be underrated. The crimes of the statesmen, such for instance as the supreme crime of the continuance of the blockade after the end of hostilities, are in a very real sense the crimes of the nations which they represent. But this popular responsibility is of a limited character. The power of the modern state machinery, above all its control over information, and its almost boundless power of subtle propaganda, leaves the public with hardly any defence against deception. Under modern democratic conditions, the statesmen must, in the common phrase, "carry the nation with them"; and what this means in practice is that a new department of Government activity, that of propaganda, has been developed to meet the need.

Incidents occasionally occur which show to what extent nations are responsible for the things done in their name. The plain man is now and then brought face to face with realities, in such a way as to dispense with all need of imagination, and enable him suddenly to see things as they are. Such an incident was the effect of the distress of the German population upon the morale of the British army of occupation on the Rhine. The famous telegram of General Plumer to the Supreme

Council at Paris, pointing out the bad effect on his troops of the sight of women and children starving around them in the streets of Cologne—a telegram which was, in point of fact, the first step in the modification of the blockade policy—showed in a flash how differently the plain man would feel and act, if he could see through the artificial mist created by the Government and the press. It was actually found necessary to increase the food-ration for the population of the occupied districts, in order that British soldiers might cease to ask themselves uncomfortable questions.

The blindness and mental confusion of the Allied statesmen has made it impossible for them to pursue any object consistently. Even from the point of view of securing their own objects—the destruction of German militarism, and the prevention of social revolution—we can easily see that their policy has failed through sheer inability to choose the right means and adhere to them. The German people have been driven, for instance, to a condition of despair and recklessness from which they must attempt to escape, either by violent militarist reaction, or by sporadic plunges into the least considered forms of Communism. This is generally recognized as the real danger, from the Allies' point of view, in the Germany of to-day. The task of a moderate democratic Government in that country has been made an impossible one. Those who attempt it are faced with the charge that, for all their moderation and all their democracy, they are unable to secure better terms than their more showy and sensational rivals would have done. Their one chance of success would lie in their power to revive the productive forces of their country, and to show some steady progress towards reconstruction; and this possibility is precisely what the policy of the Allies has denied to them. An atmosphere is created in which the most powerful appeals can be made, either to reaction or to revolutionary excesses.

Take, again, the Allies' attempt to prevent the spread of "Bolshevism." The right course would have been to maintain a stable Germany as a moderating influence in the centre of Europe. If they wished to grind Germany to pieces, it was vain to expect that they could stem the infection of "Bolshevism" Westwards. And as to Russia herself, no one did more to promote "Bolshevism" than the Allied statesmen themselves—first in prolonging the War long after it might otherwise have been concluded; next in refusing the Kerensky Government's appeal for an Allied peace policy in accord with that of the first Russian Revolution; then in refusing to save Russia, by joining in the negotiations, from the humiliation of Brest-Litovsk (March 1918); lastly, and above all, by treating a movement largely due to misery and despair with further doses of misery and despair, administered by the blockade, the destruction of industry, the fomenting of civil war, and the more direct processes of military and naval invasion.

These are only a few examples among many of the failure of the Allied rulers to adapt means to ends. The chief feature of the German and Austrian Treaties of Peace is that two wholly incompatible objects are pursued—the extraction of a huge indemnity, which could only be paid by industrially prosperous states, and side by side with this, the destruction of the economic fabric which alone could render possible the payment of the indemnity. Another inconsistency is that which marked the policy pursued towards the Hungarian Communist Government. At one and the same moment, in the summer of 1919, the Allies were urging the neighbouring states to a great military onslaught, and sending General Smuts to negotiate peace.

In the Baltic states, again, they pursued an extraordinary policy of vacillation towards the German troops. The story is one which, had it not been a scene in the greatest tragedy of history, might have provided a suitable theme for comic opera. General Von der Golz's forces, which defied the German Government, and supported the reactionary Baltic nobility, were looked upon with alternate favour and disfavour. By the Armistice terms (November 1918) they were to be retained in the Baltic states until the Allies should decide that the time for their withdrawal had come. In other words, they were treated as allies in the anti-Bolshevist campaign. They were neither molested nor reproved. Only after seven months (June 1919) were they ordered to withdraw; and then no serious attempt was made to enforce the order. The Lettish Government was encouraged by the Allies to accept their aid, in return for which it promised rights of citizenship to the German soldiers, one of whose chief motives was to find a method of escape from a starving and hopeless Germany. In April 1919 these forces effected a *coup d'état*, and placed a Baltic barons' Government in power at Libau; this Government was overthrown by pressure from the Allies. In May they captured Riga; in July they were driven out by an improvised Lettish force; this was on the point of crushing them, when the Allies intervened, requested the Letts to allow the Germans to retire into Courland, and imposed an armistice which enabled them to escape destruction. As the summer wore on, the orders to withdraw became more peremptory, and culminated in an ultimatum in September, backed by the threat of reimposing the starvation blockade against Germany if General Von der Golz did not withdraw.

The fact was that the Allied statesmen could never make up their minds whether they were more afraid of the General and his militarists, of the Red Army from Russia, which the General and his anti-Bolshevist Russian allies might help to resist, or of the Communist element among the Lettish population. Their decisions fluctuated from time to time, according as the one or the other consideration was uppermost in their minds—according as the Bolshevist front swayed Eastwards or Westwards.

German soldiers were employed to keep "order" whenever it was necessary, not only in the Baltic states, but also in the Ukraine during the "Bolshevist" régime of Rakovsky in the early part of 1919. Mr. Churchill, whose thoughts were directed rather to the living war with Russia than to the defunct war with Germany, even bestowed praises upon German military power as a bulwark against the dreaded irruption from Moscow. The small border states did not know from moment to moment what treatment to expect. They might be condemned to-day as "pro-German," and reprieved to-morrow as "anti-Bolshevist."

2. Phrases and Realities.

The mental confusion which has produced such inconsistencies has been largely due to the peculiar conditions under which the rulers of "democratic" states have to conduct their policy. The traditions of the old diplomacy, limited and immoral as they were, were at least free from ambiguity, from illusion, and from cant. The statesmen of earlier wars—a Richelieu, a Pitt, or a Bismarck—could "ride in the whirlwind and direct the storm" with serene self-confidence and consistency. But the necessities of modern democracy require that the aims of conquest shall be glozed over with phrases. The hands may be the hands of Esau, but the voice must always be the voice of Jacob. A statesman who is not a great man becomes confused by the unnatural atmosphere in which he works. He mistakes the phrases for the realities. The Allied statesmen have to a certain extent deceived themselves as well as others; as when President Wilson, after telling an audience of business men that the Treaty with Germany was "a good business proposition," went on to describe it as "a great enterprize, an enterprize of divine mercy and goodwill" (*Morning Post, September* 20, 1919). The more slippery they feel their moral position to be, the more hysterically they protest the purity of their motives. They live from hand to mouth. Now it is the sentiment of the moment that sways them; now the latest bugbear of the press; now the pressure of frankly Machiavellian Allies; now the financial or commercial interests of men who are cleverer than themselves, or at least act more promptly and consistently upon a simpler and narrower field.

This last is an aspect of Allied policy to which little attention has been directed. Aims of economic aggrandisement are easily concealed under high-flown phrases. The ordinary newspaper-reader hears little of them. In the commercial and financial press, however, they find plain and outspoken expression. The patient research of Mr. Walton Newbold and others has thrown a flood of light on the effort of European and American capital to safeguard its interests in Eastern Europe and Asia; on the influence of the oil interests concerned in Mesopotamia, in Persia, in the Baku region of the Caucasus, and in East Galicia; on the part played by the iron-field of Lorraine in the secret agreement of February 1917, and the natural gas area of Southern Hungary in that of August 1916; on the demands of foreign concessionnaires in the Ottoman Empire; on the connexion of French policy towards Russia with the interests of French bondholders; and on the significance of the war against Soviet Russia, in view of the gigantic industrial and commercial development of which Russia is destined to be the scene for a century to come. Following such indications, we begin to understand what might otherwise be puzzling—why the tobacco district of Bulgaria has assumed such importance in the peace negotiations; why the northern boundary of British influence is drawn from Haifa on the Palestine coast to Mosul on the Tigris, cutting the Arab nationality in two, and crossing a tractless desert; why the Ukrainians of East Galicia are handed over against their will to the more amenable Government of Poland; why the Roumanians made the River Theiss the boundary of their claims; and, above all, what it was that gave such vitality to the new war against the Russian Soviet Republic.

As each month passes, as "revelation" follows "revelation," and as the illusions of war-time begin to fade, it becomes increasingly clear that behind this susceptibility to diverse influences, this vacillation, this inefficiency, lies a moral as well as an intellectual blindness. Perhaps the most obvious instances have been the breaches of faith, of which Germany, Russia, Hungary, and the Allied people themselves, were in turn the victims. That involved in the Peace Treaty with Germany was at once the most definite in its character, and the most damaging in the eyes of the neutral world.

The Armistice Agreement of November 11, 1918, was made upon the basis of President Wilson's "Fourteen Points." It was on the faith of that Agreement that Germany laid down her arms. There was nothing ambiguous about it. On October 20th the Government of Prince Max of Baden had notified President Wilson of its willingness to make peace on the basis of the "Fourteen Points" and of the principles outlined therein and in his subsequent addresses. In response to this the Allied Governments (in a statement incorporated in the American Note of November 5th to the German Government) "declared their willingness to make peace with the Government of Germany on the terms of peace laid down in the President's Address to Congress in January 1918, and the principles of settlement enunciated in his subsequent addresses," with two specific reservations, referring to the freedom of the seas and the definition of the word "restoration." It was open to the Allies to reject the proposed basis. But they accepted it, and having done so they were bound to keep their pledges. What followed is matter of history. The Peace Treaty, as has been fully explained above, violated every one of the principles on the faith of which Germany had laid down her arms; and it was not long before the "Fourteen Points" were openly repudiated by the Allied press.

Nor was this the only breach of faith which arose out of the Armistice Agreement. By Clause 26, "The Allies and the United States contemplate the provisioning of Germany during the Armistice as shall be found necessary." The necessity was fully admitted. On November 11th, M. Clémenceau said: "As the situation of Germany and Austria is desperate, we should do all that is possible to re-victual them to such a degree as will not impoverish ourselves"; and President Wilson stated on the same day that the Allies had "assured the peoples of the Central Empires that everything possible will be done to supply them with food to relieve the distressing want that is in so many places threatening their very lives." In spite of this undertaking, however, the Allies failed even to begin to feed Germany until five months later (April 1919), and then only because British soldiers had begun to give away their rations to starving German children.

This leads on to the question of the post-War blockade as a whole. The starvation of our enemies during the War was a terrible weapon. It cost Germany some three-quarter million lives. But it was a weapon of war. The war spirit, the war psychology, the deadly fear which grips the vitals and hardens the heart—these things explain much and excuse much. But when this explanation and this excuse was wholly gone—when the enemy was broken beyond the faintest possibility of recovery—it might have been thought that ordinary humanity (not to speak of prudence) would come into play. It did not do so. The blockade, whether in its technical or its substantial form, was maintained for many months. History may be searched in vain for an injury inflicted by one section of men on another, so vast in its scale, so momentous in its consequences, and so horrible in its cold-bloodedness. The statesmen could not plead the excuse, which the man in the street could plead, that they did not know the facts about the effects of the blockade. They knew the extent of the disease and death among the women and children of the enemy countries. Mr. Churchill in the House of Commons described its effects as falling "mainly on the women and children, the old, the weak, and the poor." But they also knew that the blockade was the most powerful weapon they had for enforcing the acceptance of terms contrary to the Armistice Agreement; and their deliberate and unceasing "mobilization" of hatred had inured the mind of the public to the infliction of suffering. By means of their "atrocity" campaigns, they had carefully stimulated the flow of popular fury, whenever it showed the least sign of abating. In time, of course, this fury became an inconvenience, and they would have been glad to undo the work that they had done. But it was too late. They had called up an evil spirit which they could not exorcise.

3. The Violation of Nationality.

Perhaps, however, the aspect of Allied policy which is destined to leave the deepest impression on posterity is its betrayal of the principle of nationality. No principle was more loudly and continuously professed during the War. Moreover, even from the point of view of arresting the spread of Socialism, it would have been wise for the statesmen to encourage on every hand the idea of nationality, which emphasizes the division of peoples at the expense of the division of classes. But neither the interests of humanity, nor the far-sighted promotion of their own policy, could outweigh the narrow considerations of military and commercial aggrandisement which alone appealed to them. It is unnecessary to add here to the many examples already given of the way in which the right of national self-determination was violated. The charge is almost universally admitted, even by those who believed most firmly, both in the principle itself and in the intention of the rulers to put it into practice. The right of peoples to decide their own destiny, first raised as an inspiring war-cry, has sunk to the position of a rather stale joke.

The process of exposure had begun much earlier in the minds of those who had any power of putting two and two together. The first glaring example was the Secret Agreements. Similar agreements were probably made among the enemy Governments. The difference was that these Governments did not profess the same lofty ideals. The Allied statesmen had hardly completed the series of speeches which proclaimed the disinterested purposes of the War, before they had begun to weave a network of secret engagements wholly incompatible with those purposes. The first of these engagements (as far as is publicly known) was the promise of Constantinople to Russia (March 1915). This was followed by the Secret Treaty of London in April 1915, whereby a large German population, and a still larger South Slav population, were promised to Italy; by an agreement (in the Spring of 1916) for the partition of Turkey between Britain, France, and Russia—subsequently revised to admit Italy; by an agreement leaving the settlement of the Western frontier of Russia, including the whole fate of Russian Poland, to the Tsar (?March 1916); by an agreement with Roumania in August 1916; by various agreements dealing with Arabia, Persia, and China; and by an agreement between France and Russia (February 1917) for the detachment from Germany of the whole territory West of the Rhine. It was this disastrous series of secret engagements which prevented every attempt at a peace on the basis of self-determination and public right. They were the direct and immediate cause, both of the prolongation of the War itself, and of the internal disputes which, after the War was over, delayed the final conclusion of peace for more than a year, and destroyed the last chance of political or economic recovery in Europe.

The Germans of West Prussia and of the Saar Valley; the Austrians of Bohemia, Moravia, and South Tyrol; the Ukrainians subjected to Poland, Czechoslovakia, and Roumania; the South Slavs subjected to Italy; the Bulgarians subjected to Jugoslavia, Greece, and Roumania—these are the most conspicuous examples of a violation to which frequent allusion has been made already; and it would be tedious to repeat the tale.

It is hardly possible to realize the callous cruelty with which the weaker nations have been treated, without studying one by one the solemn promises which were made to them in the hour of need, when their support in the War was of practical importance. One or two typical examples must suffice.

The South Slav peoples oppressed by Austria were promised that they were to be redeemed at last, and were to find their national unity under the *ægis* of the Allies. This had been proclaimed in a score of speeches, and was urged, indeed, as the highest justification for the War. Yet Sir Edward Grey did not hesitate to sign on April 26, 1915, behind their backs, a Treaty with Italy which handed over 750,000 South Slavs to a Government at least as offensive to them as that of the Hapsburgs; and did so, not merely in vague terms, but with a precise demarcation of territory which was the death-knell of South Slav aspirations in Dalmatia.

Promises, again, were made to the Arabs on October 24, 1915, June 11, 1917, and November 9, 1918, which (in spite of verbal loopholes) were understood by them as promising an independent Arab state, including, *inter alia*, Mesopotamia, Palestine, and the hinterland of Syria, with such great cities as Damascus and Aleppo. The documents concerned, says Colonel Lawrence, the Englishman who carried on the negotiations with the Arabs, "were all produced under stress of military urgency to induce the Arabs to fight on our side" (*Times, September* 9, 1919). Yet, by the secret Sykes-Picot Agreement of May 1916, the whole of these territories were divided into a French and a British sphere of influence, while certain portions of them, particularly Mesopotamia, were to be annexed. As for Palestine, by the secret agreement of 1916 it was to be "subjected to a special régime to be determined by agreement between Russia, France, and England"; while yet another destination was promised for it by the letter of the British Foreign Secretary on November 9, 1917, which stated that the British Government would use its best endeavours to facilitate the establishment, in that country, of a national home for the Jews.

To turn to Georgia. The British Foreign Office, in a letter dated December 30, 1918, assured that country of its support for her claim to be heard at Paris as an independent state. On the other hand, General Denikin was opposed to Georgian independence; his design was to incorporate Georgia, with its great economic resources, in a "united and indivisible Russia"; and the British were supporting General Denikin. The Georgians, though they feared the Bolshevists, feared General Denikin still more. British hostility to Georgia gradually increased. Newspaper correspondents, recalling that Georgia had in June 1918 made peace with the Turks (and conveniently forgetting that Armenia had done the same thing, under the pressure of the same necessity), began to describe Georgia as a "product of German and Turkish strategy." The British generals accompanying General Denikin advised her on May 23, 1919, to submit to the latter's demands, allowed his troops to enter Batum, and arranged an armistice which gave into his hands the key of the Georgian territory.

An even more striking example was that of Armenia. The Armenian people had received unqualified promises of support from the British and Allied Governments. No other race had seen its sufferings more constantly or more fervently deplored in the British press. In the whole catalogue of "atrocities," none had been used with more deadly effect upon Allied and neutral opinion, as a means of arousing execration against Turkey and Germany alike, than the atrocities which were undoubtedly committed against that sorely tried people. Yet when the time came to do something practical for their cause, it appeared that no policy had been really agreed upon. No prospect of help, at any rate, was held out to them, except the vague hope that America would some day accept a mandate for their administration. The small British force to which the harassed remnant of the Armenians, in the old cradle-land of their race, looked for protection against the Tartars, Kurds, and Turks, was one of the first to be withdrawn. The British people, it is true, were clamouring for the return of their sons and brothers. But they might well have asked why, when tens of thousands of those sons and brothers were engaged in military operations in Archangel and Murmansk, in the Gulf of Kronstadt, on the Volga, in Siberia and the Far East, and even in other parts of the Caucasus itself, those selected for withdrawal should be precisely the little force which was, incidentally, rendering a humanitarian service out of all proportion to its numbers.

Let us take the case finally of China. She had been promised that her national independence would be protected in return for her entry into the War on the side of the Allies. She believed, in the words of a Chinese statesman, "that the War was something nobler than a mere war of conflicting interests." She was not destined, however, to see this belief realized when the time came for the settlement.

The Allies allowed Japan to retain Kiao-chau, which belonged to China. They are said to have consented, by secret agreements of February and March 1917, to the twenty-one economic and political demands wrung by Japan from China on May 25, 1915, including the claim to virtual possession of Shantung. In any case, they did so consent when the time came. In spite of vehement protests by the American Congress and people,

Japan's claims were maintained. China's trust in the superior morality of the Western Powers received a shock which has left permanent marks on the psychology of her people, especially on the student and merchant classes, the guiding factors in her intellectual and political life. The Chinese problem has taken a place equal in magnitude to that of the African, in the long story of the exploitation of "weaker" races by commercial imperialism.

4. The Anti-Socialist Crusade.

But if "self-determination" was violated by the subjection of unwilling peoples to foreign rule, it proved no less empty a phrase in its application to internal politics. According to democratic principle, the majority of a people has a right to the Government of its own choice; and in pursuance of that right may refuse to accept, not merely a foreign Government, but equally a Government composed of native parties or individuals of whom it disapproves. This right was completely denied by the Allies in their attitude towards the various social transformations which were now in progress. Here "self-determination" stopped short. It was not to extend to the adoption of a Socialist form of Government. Socialism thus audaciously put into practice provoked, in the minds of the statesmen, an immediate reaction which was not the less real because it was largely instinctive. This widespread assault on private property threatened the capitalist system of society—and they were not capable of conceiving any other. They reacted no less violently against the international doctrines of Socialism. The new movement threatened the political as well as the social system—the system of national states, sovereign, independent, self-contained. The propagandists of Socialism preached, with varying degrees of emphasis, loyalty to a principle which transcended national divisions, and to that extent they undermined allegiance to the national cause.

"Bolshevist propaganda" became the special bugbear of the Allied statesmen. They represented it as an aggressive interference by one state in the affairs of another, and therefore a justification for retaliatory measures. This aspect of it, however, though it provided them with a useful pretext, was not the real ground of their opposition. Interference in the affairs of other states was a habitual part of their own practice. What roused their nervous apprehension was the particular character of the propaganda. It was subversive of the whole political and social world in which they lived and moved.

The main form which their opposition to Socialism assumed was the war against Soviet Russia, begun in June 1918 on a small scale (mainly under the pretext of resisting German penetration into Russia) and developing rapidly in scope and intensity. The nature of this conflict and its far-reaching consequences have already been described in our third chapter. Here it is only necessary to refer shortly to certain aspects of it which throw a light on the attitude of the statesmen who conducted it. There were, of course, differences of opinion among them; and these centred chiefly round the practical questions whether the Soviet Government should be recognized, whether negotiations should be entered into, and whether the troops of this or that Ally should be withdrawn.

A section of the statesmen desired to recognize the Lenin Government and make peace with it. They secured in February 1919 the proposal of a Conference at Prinkipo, in the Sea of Marmora, between the various warring authorities of Russia. The Communists accepted the conditions, while their opponents refused. No advantage, however, was taken of this proof—which was one of many—of a readiness to make peace. The warlike counsels always prevailed in the end. It was only by the most shameless subterfuges that this refusal of all negotiation, this war *á outrance*, could be justified to the peoples of the Entente. The most vivid light on the conflicting currents, and the invariable predominance of the anti-Socialist influences, was thrown by the evidence of Mr. Bullitt before the Foreign Relations Committee of the American Senate. Mr. Bullitt had been a high official in the American Peace Mission at Paris, and was widely known and trusted. In February 1919 he was sent to Russia, on the suggestion of Mr. Lansing and Colonel House, to ascertain what terms of peace the Soviet Government would accept. Before starting, he received from Mr. Lloyd George's secretary an unofficial outline of the British terms ; while Mr. Lloyd George offered a British cruiser to convey him on his mission. He came back with a set of terms which were regarded as reasonable, even by anti-Bolshevist circles. His report was sent to President Wilson by the Secretary of State, Mr. Lansing, marked "urgent." It was also discussed by Mr. Bullitt at luncheon with Mr. Lloyd George, who urged Mr. Bullitt to publish it, though President Wilson opposed publication. On April 16th Mr. Lloyd George, asked in the House of Commons whether there had been any "approaches" or "representations" from Russia, gave a reply which was so framed as to convey to the public that no authentic terms had been received; though he guarded himself by adding that none had been brought before the Peace Conference "by any member of that Conference." His references to Mr. Bullitt and his mission were as follows: "I have only heard of reports that others have got proposals which they assume have come from authentic quarters. . . . I think I know what the right hon. gentleman refers to. There was some suggestion that there was some young American who had come back. All I can say about that is that it is not for me to judge the value of such communications." Mr. Lloyd George, while describing Mr. Bullitt's statement as a "tissue of lies," abstained from denying that he had discussed the terms with that gentleman on his return.

On the question of the withdrawal of Allied forces from Russia, there was throughout 1919 the same confusion of counsel, and the same failure on the part of the moderating influences to control the course of policy. A single incident will provide a better illustration than a long narrative of decisions, counter-decisions, deceptions, and compromises. In September 1919 it was officially announced to the British press representatives in Paris that the Supreme Council had decided to leave Soviet Russia to work out its own salvation. The decision was promptly denied by the French, American, and Italian peace missions. A controversy raged for some time in the press. It was at last brought to an end on September 19th by the following explanation, given officially to the Exchange Telegraph Company: "According to the best information I was able to obtain to-day the exact facts are as follows: Close upon 12.30 on Monday, at the end of the meeting of the Council of Five, and after the Allied statesmen had been engaged in a serious discussion of Roumanian and Serbian questions and the effects which might accrue from D'Annunzio's 'raid' on Fiume, Mr. Lloyd George, as he was about to leave the Conference Chamber, turned to his colleagues and remarked, 'What about the Russian question? I think you will agree with me that we have had enough of this Russian expedition. I think we had better let the Russians alone to look after their own affairs.' No word of dissent was spoken by the other delegates, who presumably did not realize the importance of the question."

A News Agency was informed at Downing Street the same evening that "There is not anything to add to what has already been said upon the matter. It is, after all, the policy which matters, and that policy has not altered in the least from that announced recently by the Minister for War."

5. The Failure of Wilsonism.

We have seen how the Allied Governments, which had entered the war as the champions of democracy and of nationality, betrayed their high-sounding promises, and disappointed the generous hopes which those promises had excited. The idealism which had glowed in their speeches was gradually exposed by the searching light of cold facts. Some branded it as a deception; others dismissed it as a pathetic illusion; all alike, whether with triumph or with regret, recognized that it had failed to influence the course of events.

The familiar principles which had governed the settlements of 1815, of 1856, and of 1871 had been asserted once more—with some slight concessions, it is true, to the democratic aspirations of the new generation, but without any fundamental change of spirit. The statesmen, following the grooves of the old diplomacy, unrestrained by any effective public criticism, and steeped in the prejudice of class, had conceived the whole situation along the only lines which they could understand and appreciate. Their eyes were blind to the larger interests of mankind. They did not realize that wrongs done to Germany or Russia, to Hungary or Bulgaria, were merged in the greater injury to humanity, including, of course, the injury to ourselves. They were not great enough to call a halt in the process of destruction, in order to preserve or reconstruct the indispensable basis for the civilization of the future. They lived in a world of out-of-date ideas, impervious to the breath of the new time. In an age when an appreciable portion of the human race was threatened by death with starvation, and in the presence of the greatest social revolution, perhaps, of all time, they could offer no more inspiring guidance to the anxious and tormented peoples than the old catchwords of "crushing Germany" and "crushing Bolshevism." They had in point of fact destroyed neither Militarism nor Socialism. But they had destroyed the belief that bourgeois democracy contained within it any living force that could regenerate the world.

No group among the statesmen bears a heavier responsibility than those who, by their liberal or democratic attitude of mind, attached to the proceedings of Paris a certain respectability. It was they who induced the peoples to accept all manner of evils, such as the iniquities of the post-war blockade, in the belief that the liberal and democratic statesmen constituted a guarantee that these things would not be done without absolute necessity, and that justice would prevail in the end. It was a curiously assorted group of statesmen who together cast this glamour over the Peace Conference—Lord Robert Cecil, General Smuts, Mr. Vandervelde, Mr. Lloyd George, President Wilson. None of these men saw that, under the circumstances, protests made in the course of secret negotiations were futile. Nothing short of resignation and a complete abjuration of the Peace Conference, with all the admitted dangers which such a course might have entailed, could possibly have met the case. Their "staying in" not only rendered their efforts vain, but rendered tolerable a series of proceedings which ought to have been arrested at any cost, because they were incapable of being readjusted on lines of morality. Liberal ideas proved to be nothing more than a narcotic—a practical device for soothing troubled consciences. When, after the outlines of the Peace Treaties were drawn, some of these men tried to justify their conduct by public protests, it was too late. The thing was done. The world was faced with the naked outcome of the War.

The effects of the exposure of the Wilsonian ideology were immense. Those who had always disbelieved in it, found in its exposure an occasion for rejoicing. "Bolshevism" has no more precious asset than the failure of "Capitalist Society" to put its professions into practice. But the consequences were not confined to the strengthening of critics and opponents.

The confidence reposed in President Wilson had been so genuine, so deep, and so widespread, both among the Allied and the enemy peoples, that when it was shattered, it seemed as if all faith in justice and disinterestedness was shattered at the same time. The victorious peoples, tired of the War and its distractions, accepted apathetically the accomplished fact. The beaten peoples sank into despair. But both sides alike drifted more and more into an attitude of general scepticism, of contempt for the "ideals" which had proved so sterile. The feelings of those who had accepted the Wilsonian speeches as interpreting the aims of the Allies, were poignantly expressed in a letter written by Mr. Bullitt to President Wilson, on resigning his post in the American Peace Commission. After pointing out in detail the injustice and the danger of the settlement imposed by the Paris Conference, the letter concluded :—

"That you are personally opposed to most of the unjust settlements, and that you accepted them only under great pressure, is well known. Nevertheless, it is my conviction that if you had made your fight in the open instead of behind closed doors, you would have carried with you the public opinion of the world, which was yours. You would have been able to resist this pressure, and might have established that 'new international order based upon broad and universal principles of Right and Justice' of which you used to speak.

"I am sorry you did not fight our fight to a finish, and that you had so little faith in the millions of men like myself in every nation who had faith in you."

CHAPTER VII

BELOW THE TIDE OF WAR

Gentleness, Virtue, Wisdom and Endurance,
These are the seals of that most firm assurance
Which bars the pit over Destruction's strength. . . .
These are the spells by which to reassume
An empire o'er the disentangled doom.

SHELLEY.

1. The Signs of Recovery.

WE have been compelled to paint a picture in which the sombre colours predominate. But this does not mean that no hopeful signs are discernible in the welter that surrounds us. What it means is that the values, which these signs represent, belong to the future rather than to the present; and it is the events of the present that we have tried to depict.

Those events leap to the eye, and fill the scene. What we have to say about the signs of recovery must necessarily seem slight, in comparison with the solid facts with which we have been mainly concerned—the breaking up of empires, the shiftings of power, the volcanic social upheavals. The voice of hope appears strangely small and still, after the rocking earthquake and the devastating fire.

Yet these new forces are not to be ignored. The efforts of many men in the official world, despite the pressure or the inertia of their superiors, to modify the worst features of Allied policy; the concessions which the statesmen have been compelled to make, here and there, to popular ideas of humanity or democracy; the works of relief and reconstruction which are beginning on all hands, and in which friends, enemies, and neutrals co-operate; the patient work of such bodies as the Committee for the Resumption of International Relations in France, the Union of Democratic Control in Britain, and the New Fatherland Society in Germany; these things are seeds from which recovery and reconciliation may spring. They point to the possibility that, even within the limits of the political system which we have seen to be establishing itself, some improvements in the present confusion and distress may be effected. The machinery of the League of Nations may be utilized to revise the Treaties of Peace. The more brutal of the economic and financial provisions, after serving the purpose of providing an apparent fulfilment of the statesmen's promises, may be quietly dropped or modified. Under the pressure of economic distress a popular demand may arise for the removal of unnecessary burdens, both in the matter of tariffs and trade restrictions, and in the matter of armaments. The policy of disarmament appeals to popular traditions and instincts in Britain and America. Profiteering in armaments, and the cynical subordination of patriotism to money-making in that most powerful of industries, provide ample material for the anti-militarist campaign of which there are already signs in every European country.

The pressure of economic facts will operate in

an even more direct manner to draw the peoples together. There will be a period of high prices and of unemployment, with revolutionary consequences varying in degree in different countries. The failure to revive the industry of Central and Eastern Europe will be seen to be the root cause of the trouble. No indemnity will be forthcoming which will not be more than outweighed by the losses sustained in gaining it. The victorious peoples will find that they have to bear their burdens themselves. The hope of shifting them on to other shoulders will gradually fade away. It will be borne in upon them by the hard logic of suffering that nations are interdependent; that, if the world is to live at all, it must live by co-operation; that the hope of gaining something by destroying other peoples was a disastrous illusion. Some form of international economic organization for distributing the necessities of life and industry according to the need, rather than the mere capacity to pay, will become inevitable. It will form the most real and practical element in the League of Nations.

2. International Socialism.

The gradual growth of International Socialism provides another ground of hope. The divisions of language, the difficulties of travel for the poor man, the differences of method, of custom, and of circumstances in the various countries, render its growth inevitably slow. They are still being artificially emphasised by the barriers imposed by the Governments, censorship, the refusal of passports, the misrepresentation of one people in the eyes of another. These obstacles are counterbalanced, however, by the growing self-consciousness of Labour in all countries. The abiding strength of the International Socialist movement, whether united in one organization or pursuing different paths towards the same goal of social transformation, is that it stands for a common interest and a common demand. It sees a real conflict of interests between classes, but not between nations. It holds that the working classes of the different countries, unlike the Governments, should have no claims which are incompatible with one another ; their real needs can all be harmonized. This is the solid economic foundation with which the genius of Marx replaced the Utopianism of earlier Socialists. It gives to internationalism a simple and intelligible basis. It is a fact which will be more and more clearly realized as the years go on. International Socialism is the only international force which has a definite, a practical, and a generally known policy for dealing with the troubles of the time. It is the only international force which effectively transcends national divisions. Even the conflicts within its own ranks, such as that between the " Bolshevists " and the " anti-Bolshevists," cut across the antagonisms of race and nationality, and unite the enemies of yesterday in defence of a common cause. The real Society of Nations will be born when the peoples can speak to one another through Socialist Governments, that is to say, through Governments which repudiate the principle of national self-assertion, and place the social welfare first. The germ of such a Society is to be found in the International Socialist movement of to-day.

But we must go deeper. The change of economic and political forms is only real and substantial when it takes place concurrently with a revolution of thought. Neither part of the process is complete without the other; the ideas affect the outward forms, but it is no less true that the outward forms react upon the ideas. Of the two, the changes in thought are the more fundamental.

3. The Revolt of Youth.

We turn, then, to certain manifestations of thought which, remote as they may seem at first sight from the subjects we have hitherto discussed, and small as the space may be which they occupy for the moment in the eyes of statesmen, nevertheless are in reality, and in the long run, more rich in hope and promise than the external changes with which we have up to now concerned ourselves. Bruised reed and smoking flax though they may be, the true servant of humanity will seek them out and cherish them. The human spirit has a life of affection and of thought which cannot be altogether crushed. It persists, undestroyed if not undisturbed, below the tide of war which sweeps over it; and here and there it rises in conscious revolt against the trammels and the insults which the conditions of war impose upon it. Such a revolt is that which has led to the innumerable protests, in the name of youth, against the domination of the old—protests passing through the whole scale of emotion, from contemptuous cynicism to passionate indignation. The world of 1914 is felt to have been in the hands of men whose minds moved along fixed grooves; men whose reputations had been built up, not by merit, but by the mere passage of time; men who, without fighting themselves, urged others to fight, and enjoyed the excitement of the War at second-hand.

The protest has welled up spontaneously and independently in the heart of those great nations which form the main sources of European culture —Britain, France, and Germany. In Britain it has found much vigorous expression in journalism and in poetry. In France it is well typified in the group of young artists and writers who gather round such reviews as *La Forge* and *Clarté*. In Germany it has taken shape in a bewildering variety of organizations and groups, such as the "Free German League of Youth" and the "Free Socialist Youth of Germany," with all their apparatus of journals and of conferences. At bottom, the movement is an assertion of the claim of youth to life and freedom; the keen consciousness of individuality, which refuses to regard itself as fodder for cannon, doomed by some senseless fate to expiate the stupidity of the old. It tends to become a conscious effort of the individual to think out his relationship to society and to the state, unfettered by the traditions of the past or the prejudices of the present. It is of its essence that it has no recognized leaders. It swears allegiance to no master. Yet it looks with affectionate enthusiasm towards the men of thought who kept their heads during the War—men such as Rolland, Barbusse, Wilhelm Förster, Bertrand Russell, Lowes Dickinson—none of them, be it noted, over middle age.

4. The International of Thought.

The International of Thought, represented by such names as these, played but a small part while the War was in progress. Nor do its ideas spread quickly; for the "intellectual" who has been swept off his feet and has consciously accepted the position of the unthinking majority, still remains a man of ideas; he does not shift his ground with the ease of the uneducated mind, which grasps ideas more loosely. But there are signs that the world of science and of art is moving steadily, if slowly, towards the position occupied by such men as those just mentioned.

These men are making a conscious effort to rally the forces of reason and humanity by means of the written and the spoken word. The mind, they say, has been prostituted to the service of a narrow nationalism; but in reality it should know no frontiers. It must recover itself. It must resume the disinterested search for truth. And truth is not to be found in a cloistered seclusion. It is to be pursued for a practical end, the interest of all humanity. The International of Thought has the duty of championing the cause of human freedom on the intellectual and moral battlefield.

It is of great significance that the clearest and most conscious statement—or restatement—of this inspiring conception has come from France—that France which has been in the modern world the supreme originator of ideas, the intellectual mother of Europe. Romain Rolland gave voice to it at the very outset of the War in his *Au-dessus de la Mêlée.* Henri Barbusse, who followed later in

Rolland's steps, is perhaps even more typical of the time. He served in the trenches, and depicted in *Le Feu* the ghastly realities through which he had lived. Only gradually, and by direct experience, was he led to his attitude of conscious protest, first against the ideas which had made the War possible, and then against the ideas which make the present social system possible. In his articles and manifestoes, and above all in his later novel *Clarté*, which has given its name to an international organization formed to promote the ideas it expresses—we see the French intellect unifying and systematizing what might otherwise have been a bundle of vague aspirations. " Youth is the true force," says Barbusse, " but it is too seldom lucid."

Barbusse believes in no external revelation, but he believes that " truth is within the heart of man," that life is sacred, and that the moral law is self-evident. He vigorously asserts the free will of the individual, and his responsibility for the collective life. An artist who keeps himself apart from the interests and concerns of the masses—" the People, constituted by all the peoples "—is no longer a true artist. He must " turn towards the living multitudes, to encourage, to teach, to defend, to unite." He must play his part in the great war of ideas which underlies all the conflicts, both social and national, of the age we live in. The triumph of reason and humanity is possible. The honest presentment of truth will enable us to see things without the illusions of sentiment. Night surrounds us ; but we have this advantage—" we know whereof the night is made." Truth will reveal to us who and what we are; it will reveal to us those whom we have been told to hate, as souls in trouble and confusion like ourselves. It will break down the barriers which shut out love and human pity, and the understanding which pardons all. Just as human thought has produced the progress that we have hitherto attained, so human thought can end war, and build up the creative society of the future.

This rallying of the thinkers and artists of Europe is destined to have a slow but sure effect, undermining the older conception of patriotism, discrediting the "ancestral voices" which rise within us from out of the sub-liminal memories of the race, focussing our speculation upon the realities and the possibilities. More and more it is colouring the minds of those who, though now a minority in numbers, and filling subordinate positions, are destined by their vigour and independence of mind to influence events ten or twenty years hence—the journalists, teachers, and writers of the rising generation.

5. A New Religion?

No mention has hitherto been made of religion. So far as the organized churches are concerned, we believe that no impartial observer could look on them as likely to play any important part in the healing of the nations and the creation of a new society. The individual exceptions among them—and above all the high-souled but unsuccessful efforts of Pope Benedict XV—have been too few to redeem them from the charge of ineffectiveness. It is not that they have failed to apply, in a pagan world, the more extreme and paradoxical of the precepts of Jesus. That, perhaps, would have been too much to ask. The charge is that, on both sides alike, they hounded the nations on to fight; that, in spite of the powerful influence they wielded in every country, they failed to mitigate the cruelties of the War, even where (as in the persecution of enemy aliens) these cruelties had no military excuse; that they failed to purify the peace settlement which followed it from the spirit of conquest and vengeance; that they raised no effective protest even against the deliberate starvation of the enemy peoples after their military resistance had been crushed. The noble agnosticism of the "intellectuals" who fought against the war-spirit, the crude materialism which forms the accepted creed of Continental Socialists—these proved, in point of fact, to be firmer foundations for regenerative effort than did "official" Christianity.

Yet these, too, have failed. Both materialism and agnosticism have performed immense services in the spheres of protest, of negation, of emancipation. It is on the positive side that they seem wanting. There are aspects of life of which they give no account, but of which, we believe, some account could be given, and would be given by a more comprehensive philosophy. "Think other thoughts," says Mr. Dickinson, "love other loves, Youth of England and of the world!" But what thoughts? What loves?

The War has not altered the facts of life, but it has illuminated some of them with startling clearness. The chief of these is the futility of force to produce moral improvement; its power to destroy, its impotence to create. This is the deepest spiritual lesson of the War. Any really complete account of things must explain it as a phenomenon, must connect it with the facts of psychology, must point out its consequences in the sphere of morals. It seems to us to have far-reaching implications. We do not claim to have explored them. Yet we believe that, if explored and realized, they would form the basis for a re-birth of religion. It would be a new application, or to speak more correctly the first complete application, of the teachings of Jesus—the first, because mankind has never yet accepted in practice the preliminary conditions on which He promised power to His disciples. It would be an expression of religion in deeds.

If we were to examine a possibility so momentous as this, we should be carried far beyond the limits we have laid down. This book itself, with its description of the havoc made by the attempt to solve the world's problems by force, might be regarded as the introduction, or prolegomena, to such a study.

Yet some allusion to the subject is not out of place, because signs are not wanting, even now, in the spoken or written words of contemporary men and women, of a development of thought in this new direction. One of the psychological effects of the War, as we have seen in discussing "Bolshevism," has been a strengthening of the belief in violence. But it is also true that upon a smaller number of minds, and those the most sensitive, its effect has been the opposite. It has produced a deeper reaction—an intellectual questioning of the fundamental assumptions on which the War and the peace settlement were alike based—a disbelief in force, whether force be frankly accepted as good in itself, or exercised in the name of disinterestedness, to benefit its victims. To such minds the essential falsity of the principle of force seems confirmed by the very act that, in the long run, it infallibly brings those who employ it to destruction. Our civilization, which is based upon it, seems to them to be in process of committing suicide.

Our picture would be defective if it failed to include this profound spiritual experience, which is actually taking place before our eyes as a direct outcome of the War. However small its extent at the moment, it may be the grain of mustard seed from which a mighty growth is destined to spring. Its most conscious and traceable form is that which it has taken within the ranks of the "anti-militarist" movement. Men whose names are hardly known, and whose actions are for the most part unrecorded, have experienced a new revelation. In belligerent countries such as Germany or Austria, where "conscientious objection" was not recognized, they have paid the penalty of their opinions, in an unknown number of cases, with their lives. They have refused on principle to kill their fellow-men, and under a military code by which so strange an offence was not recognized, they have been shot for "desertion" or "cowardice." In Britain and America, many of them have been exposed to contempt, misrepresentation, long terms of imprisonment, and gross ill-usage. The fact remains that they have discovered in themselves a new power, before which the ordinary methods of forcible compulsion have completely failed. Again and again the military authorities charged with the custody of "conscientious objectors" have fallen back puzzled and paralyzed, pleading in desperation for the removal of these dangerous enthusiasts out of sight and hearing of the Army. When the story of what some of these men have endured is fully known, when the reasons why they endured it are appreciated, and the mist of misrepresentation is cleared away, their action will exert a far-reaching influence, not only in the world of politics, but in the world of thought. A deed done is more potent than many words.

Such a revival as this would be no vague religion of humanity, formed by the slow paring away of untenable beliefs on this side or that. It would be a revolution. It would affect the very roots of human conduct. It would probably come in the form of a discovery, a sudden enlightenment, a catastrophic "transvaluation of values." The citizen would forget his pride of patriotism, the rich man would voluntarily renounce his material comfort. Friend and foe, rich and poor, would abandon the inveterate habit of "judging" other men, which poisons their relationships and curses even their acts of kindness, and which the founder of Christianity singled out as wholly incompatible with the life which he preached.

Yet the ideal would not be negative, but positive. These renunciations would not be felt as losses, but as means to strength, to courage, and to efficiency. It would be an abandonment of death to gain life—life without flaw, endowed with new properties and powers, the physical blossoming with the spiritual; a new consciousness of cleanness, health, and power. Unsuspected stores of energy would be released, overflowing the channels of organized religion as did the energy of Francis of Assisi or George Fox.

The question of the possibility of such a revival is a momentous one. On the answer to it would seem to depend the whole destiny of European civilization as we know it. If no such revival takes place, it is difficult to see how a whole series of violent conflicts can be prevented. The most that can be expected is the localization of these conflicts, through the machinery of a League of Nations keeping watch over Europe in the interests of a few great states. The national struggles of which, as we have seen, the seeds have been so thickly sown by the Peace Treaties and the after-War policy, will be fought out on the old lines—sometimes by actual war, sometimes by that "war of steel and gold" in which rival potentialities of strength are pitted against one another, behind a veil of diplomatic formalities. The social struggle will pass from one stage of embitterment to another, breaking here and there into armed revolution. The "Reds" and the "Whites" will not be essentially different. Both alike will appeal, in the last resort, to the same arbitrament of force. On the side of the oppressed and defeated there will be the sullen resentment which looks forward, secretly or openly, to the day of revenge. On the other side, the success secured and maintained by force will not bring the satisfaction or the well-being that was hoped from it. The injustice of the Paris Conference and the injustice of social privilege—the wrong done to the beaten enemy and the wrong done to the exploited class—will bring their own Nemesis in their train. It may not come, though often enough it will come, in the shape of a dramatic retribution. It will certainly come in moral paralysis and inward disquiet, in failure of life, in the baffling of the search for happiness.

If, on the other hand, inspired by the new conception of human values, men should begin to challenge the actual course of affairs as we see it to-day—if they were to ask themselves whether the customary conduct of life could be reconciled with that new conception—human affairs might take a wholly new direction. Vast changes would certainly take place in the political and economic spheres with which we have been concerned in the preceding chapters.

Leaving the greatest of these changes to be dealt with last, we must not ignore the fears which the "practical" man is likely to feel in contemplating so disturbing a change. Much that he has accepted as natural or indispensable would have to be transformed, and many accustomed conceptions uprooted.

It must be admitted that the immediate effect upon material production might be serious. There would be less reliance upon organization and government, and a tendency, perhaps, towards a voluntary Communism, which for the time being would be less efficient than the old system in productive power. A corresponding fall in production might take place as a result of the abandonment of that commercial exploitation of "weaker" races which is at present the chief motive force in world-politics. It would cause, probably, the persistence of what we now regard as "backwardness" in many parts of the world—China, India, Africa—which are now in the tight grip of a restless and pushing capitalism. Both at home and abroad, economic development might very possibly slacken its pace.

But there would be immediate compensations. Side by side with any deficiency in material supplies, there would be a reduction in material wants. There would be a decline in the strength of the "possessive" impulses, and a new calling forth of the "creative." Men would cease to make "the abundance of the things which he possesses" the sole test either of a man's or of a nation's welfare. Such things would be taken more lightly—shall we perhaps say, more humorously? The tragic seriousness with which they are now regarded would be insensibly dissolved. Life would be somewhat more adventurous. The War itself has done something to make such a change less alarming. We have all become more accustomed to risk than we were before. It is easier than of old to accept the Christian life—which is, at bottom, a life of adventure, and is only difficult in proportion as men become dependent upon certainty and regularity in material things.

The greatest, however, of all the effects of the new religious revival would be that which it would exercise upon the great conflicts, national and social, which during the past five years have reduced the world to chaos. These conflicts, which now seem so natural and inevitable, would yield to the solvent influences of the new faith. "No idea is so practical," says Bertrand Russell, "as the idea of the brotherhood of man, if only people could be startled into believing it," if only it were inaugurated "with the faith and vigour belonging to a new revolution." Nor is the reconciliation of classes less practically attainable than the reconciliation of nations.

Neither of these two great conflicts, in the last resort, can in any real sense be settled by the appeal to force. They can and ought to be settled by reason and concession. But this does not mean that their solution lies in a mere compromise, a process of negotiation in which each side yields something to the other as part of a bargain.

It means something much greater and deeper than this. It means the recognition that, in point of fact, there is nothing to bargain about; that the material things which formed the subjects of dispute were not things of importance, were not the things that mattered. It means the voluntary abandonment of all domination by one man, or one group of men, over another; the free and unconditional renunciation, by the possessing class or the dominant nation, of its material privilege or superiority, and by the subservient class or the subservient nation of all its resentment and all its thoughts of revenge. And here again, as in the case of the individual, the renunciation would be conceived as a gain, not as a sacrifice. For life in the real sense of the word would be seen to be concerned with other values. Effort and emulation and competition would be concentrated upon the things of the mind and the spirit—the true, the noble and the beautiful—things whose possession by one does not exclude their possession by another, and which grow greater and richer in proportion as they are shared.

Battleships and guns, guarded frontiers and colonial monopolies, the amassing of wealth and the privilege of power, all alike would be cast down from their pedestal as the deities of the modern age, the ruling forces of the world. They would be revealed as wisps of straw in the face of the new spiritual forces, the recovery of life, the

> One common wave of Thought and Joy
> Lifting mankind again.

Across the Blockade

BY HENRY NOEL BRAILSFORD

Cr. 8vo. Limp Cloth. *2s. 6d. net.*

This book records impressions formed during four months spent in blockaded Europe between February and May 1919. In Communist Hungary—In Hunger-stricken Austria—Hunger and Revolution in Vienna—A Dead City in Poland—On the Margin of Russia—The Polish Jews—Poland as Barrier—Impression of Germany—The Soviet Idea in Germany—The New Militarism—A Comment on the Peace; these are the chapter headings, and indicate the remarkable interest of the book.

Balkan Problems and European Peace

BY NOEL BUXTON AND C. LEONARD LEESE

Crown 8vo. *4s. 6d. net.*

In this book the authors trace the origins of the peoples of the Peninsula, and describe the rise of nationalism in the Balkans and its interplay with the foreign policies of the Great Powers. In elucidating the influence of these factors upon recent events, they make an important contribution to the diplomatic history of certain phases of the War. The later chapters deal with the settlement and the future. The general principles—national and international in character—which must be followed if the Balkans are to cease to be "the powder-magazine of Europe" are considered, and the details of their application outlined.

Documents and Statements relating to Peace Proposals and War Aims (Dec. 1916—1918)

INTRODUCTION BY G. LOWES DICKINSON.

Demy 8vo. *8s. 6d. net.*

The object of this publication is to preserve the record of the aims of the belligerent Governments, as set forth by them during the war in official Notes and in speeches. The choice of speeches is necessarily arbitrary, but an attempt has been made to select those which are most significant and important.

"An absolutely invaluable collection."—*Common Sense.*

The Idea of Public Right

Being the first four Prize Essays in each of the three divisions of *The Nation* Essay Competition

WITH AN INTRODUCTION BY THE RT. HON. H. H. ASQUITH.

Demy 8vo. *8s. 6d. net.*

"The essay by Mr. Emile Burns is rightly accorded the first place in the volume, and will take its place at once amongst the few outstanding examples of constructive thinking which the war has produced."—*Cambridge Magazine.*